THE MAN WHO THOUGHT OUTSIDE THE BOX

THE MAN WHO

THOUGHT OUTSIDE THE BOX

The life and times of Doctor Who Creator Sydney Newman

RYAN DANES

DIGITAL ENTROPHY

Copyright © 2017 Ryan Danes

All rights reserved

Cover design by Mark Schlesinger

Book interior design by Dallas Jones

Editors: Rick Cowdrey, Paul Gilbert, Dallas Jones

No part of this book may be reproduced or transmitted in any form or by any means, electronic or mechanical, including an information storage and retrieval system without express written permission from the author. The only exception is for a reviewer who may quote brief excerpts in a review.

Visit our website at www.digitalentropy.co.uk

Printed in the United Kingdom

First Edition: April 2017

Second Edition: November 2017

ISBN – 13 978-0-9930942-1-7

Thanks go out to my fiancée Rebecca Rowell,
my children Talliah and Seraya, and to my family for helping
make this book a reality.

Thanks also to: The Newman Estate, The National Film Board of Canada for the use of their photos, The Canadian Broadcasting Corporation, The Canadian Nation Archives, Rick Cowdery, Dallas Jones, Mark Schlesinger, Jeph Preece, Ted Kotcheff, Alvin Rakoff, Stef Coburn, Sir Michael Grade, Jonathan Powell, Elstree Studios, Peter Ware at Doctor Who Magazine, Ed Fortune, Doctor Who online, John Freeman@downthetubes, Ian Wheeler of DWAS, Jack David & ECW, Ron Mallett, Ramona Schnitger, David Havers, Steve Stotts, Adam Bunch, Alan Hunting, Gareth Kavaghner, Donna Davies, Sean Farnell, Paul Driscoll, Ian O'Brien, Chris Irving, Robert Spitz Jones, Sam Way, Patrick McKeown, Brett Harrison, Paul Rowe, Darren Morrison, K. Dando, Earl Ecklund, Jason Elford, Richard Gurl, Paul Gilbert and Ian Riley (Happy 50th birthday).

In Memory of my grandparents Joan & Percy.

THE MAN WHO THOUGHT OUTSIDE THE BOX
CONTENTS

The Police Box at the End of the Street 1
Fairy Tales and Science Fiction 14
Taking Money From the Commies 27
A Fight for Freedom and Freewill 37
Life at the NFB 46
War Films 58
New York and the Communists 68
Swapping Celluloid for Electrons 78
Time and Space 90
TV Revolution 111
Tapping a Vein 125
Armchair Avenger 136
Visiting Aunty 149
Mister Who? Doctor X? 161
Back to Canada 175
Homeward Bound 186
Becoming a Legend 196
REFERENCES 206
Afterword 210

–o 0 o–

SPECIAL EXTRA

THE TALE OF THE FOURTH STRANGER
BY ANTHONY COBURN

Introduction by Stef Coburn 205

The Tale of the Fourth Stranger 215

Chapter One
The Police Box at the End of the Street

The Gestaltists are right – the whole really is greater than the sum of its parts. The hustle and bustle of downtown Toronto during the First World War was a good example of this: a by-product of existence playing out on the sidewalks and in the boarding houses; a never-ending cycle of life going on in the apartments and churches, the pool halls and bars.

The unfortunate were dying in the trenches in France and Belgium but most back home survived by doing their best to ignore the conflict as much as they could. Hell, war was all-encompassing, so why think about it anymore than necessary? The city teetered on the brink of collapse. It could not offer the rich experiences of some places but it was far removed from the terror and destruction seen in cities like Ypres and Verdun. For the first time, ordinary people in the streets saw war and death on the newsreels, and the clever ones, like Toronto-born Sydney Cecil Newman, had his own take on the role of film.

Torontonian thinkers and creative types hung out in areas such as Queen Street West and Kensington, kids who could scrutinise something in their minds and relate its emotions to their own experiences. Beautiful concepts and symmetry emerged from this internal collision of joy and anguish; the creative mind at work. They were free-thinkers who operated outside normal conventions, bedding their work right on the edge of the acceptable and understandable. Later, some of it became mainstream and civilisation continued with a new generation running government, construction, the armed-forces and entertainment. Like today, films were one of the most popular pastimes and Sydney became enthralled by them as a boy. A few weeks after he was born, the Ontario Motion Picture Bureau, the first state-sponsored film organisation in the world, began. He would get a break with them two decades later, by which time it had evolved into the National Film Board of Canada. At the time the Second World War raged all around him, thus it was to be a baptism of fire and a chance to prove himself.

You see, I was born three blocks away at Queen and Beverley Street. Each Saturday morning, trembling with anticipation, I'd walk along Queen Street, up John Street, past the University settlement house where I got my first books I ever read, into Grange Park, and paying no attention to them because they were commonplace, past dozens and dozens of men. The unemployed washing their shirts or feet in the drinking fountain at the south end (is it still there?) or past pathetic rub-dubs, straining through a sock the last ounce of alcohol from the contents of Sterno cans or the occasional kinky guy exposing himself to the neighbourhood children. (Newman[12], 1976)

Described as *The Little Jewish boy from Queen Street (the wrong side of the Toronto Tracks)* (Vineberg, 1970) Sydney didn't lack creatively, and he showed a talent for drawing and painting from an early age, and he also modelled at the Ontario School of Art every summer for fifty cents a day (Newman[12], 1976). He was fortunate that these skills were nurtured, and then, later, his talent was recognised by his contemporaries. Where such a mind came from is anybody's guess, but there is a clear line of development throughout his early years. Representing life with such realism as a director, producer and head of department was to be the high-point of this career, but he came up against barriers – and a lady called Mary Whitehouse – along the way on more than one occasion. Sydney had a talent for getting under the skins of those on the margins of society and drawing out stories and themes, whether telling tales about teenage pregnancy in the 1950s or a mysterious alien who travelled through time and space to live in a 1963 London junkyard in his police box time-machine.

Many things inspired Sydney and there has been much speculation on how significant a role he had in the development of the show; we shall explore this in greater detail later in the book. His vision for *Doctor Who* was more than Bacofoil monsters and brains in jars, and he did not want fantastical science fiction that nobody would believe in. He knew there were loftier subjects, such as the origins of life and the formation of the universe, and that art, philosophy, and science could inspire the story-tellers to write tales that ordinary people could understand. He had been a cinema-goer since he was a young boy, and he loved to watch horror and fantasy. There had never been a better medium in which to have a voice or highlight a problem, but you had to get past those pesky censors first.

Technology moved on in leaps and bounds after the war and clear warnings for the future were evident in books like *Brave New World* (1932) by Aldous Huxley, and *1984* (1949) by George Orwell. Science was bright, shiny and new. People hoped it would end all ills. The implication of interfering with nature was a subject open for debate, and *Doctor Who* would go on to deal with ecological problems, as well as universal ones. Issues like the burning of fossil fuels and the storage of nuclear waste were big concerns to people and organisations (just as they are now) and Sydney's original idea for the show would have encouraged children to become more informed by such issues. The viewer would be left asking what had made the villain of the piece so terrible that they became a megalomaniac, rather than just accepting their insanity. At its best, *Doctor Who* achieved this during its original run and it was markedly different to Sydney's earlier creation, *The Avengers*, because the whole of time and space was up for grabs. His refusal to allow bug-eyed monsters on screen would have limited the kinds of life they could have found out there, and this would have made *Doctor Who* very different to what it had developed into by the end of William Hartnell's time on the show. Sydney would have been far more enthusiastic about Jon Pertwee's earth-bound stories in the 1970s – at least, those that did not cost the earth. After all, *The Avengers* was a tried and tested success and some of the Pertwee stories were very similar - and, of course, he knew *Doctor Who* did not have the budget to recreate *The 7th Voyage of Sinbad*.

Before *Doctor Who*, Sydney experimented with science fiction at ABC, where he produced *Target Luna*, and as a follow up the *Pathfinders* series for children.

"Newman later described Pathfinders *as a 'precursor to* Doctor Who', *and there are certainly similarities. The educational remit of the* Pathfinders *stories was also found in the earliest* Doctor Who *serials, utilising adventure storytelling to teach*

children scientific concepts (and in Doctor Who*'s case, history). The filming style is not unlike much of* Doctor Who*'s early episodes, although this is as much an artefact of its production time as anything. Many British productions of this era, particularly lower budget ones such as these, have the feel of a broadcast stage play, in contrast to the more filmic nature of the higher-end US series. As with Doctor Who,* Pathfinders *was intended for a children's audience, with enough appeal for any adults watching with them."* (Tessier, 2014)

He had been successful with this formula before and he knew what would work. It is also interesting to note the emergence of an 'electronic screwdriver' in *Pathfinders*. It is true to say Sydney did not create *Doctor Who* on his own, and that the sonic-screwdriver was not his invention, only entering the series as a regular item in the 1968 Patrick Troughton story *Fury From the Deep*. He had thought of many of the key ideas for *Doctor Who* long before Cecil Edwin Webber fleshed out his original memo on the new show, but there was no mention of such a device contained within.

A science fiction series of some sort had been in the minds of the bosses at the BBC for a number of years, and, of course, they had produced *The Quatermass Experiment* which had done well a decade before Sydney's arrival. A report had also been published on whether they should make science fiction shortly before he arrived, so he had support from within the organisation. When he finally became the Head of Drama in 1962, he was aware of the popularity of American TV shows such as *The Twilight Zone* and *Doctor Kildare*, and he had already set the pace in Britain with *The Avengers*. In the years leading up to the creation of *Doctor Who*, space exploration became big news – the first satellite Sputnik was launched in 1957 and Yuri Gagarin became the first man in space four years later. A genuine thirst for stories about science, space and the future had developed, and he wanted to tap into it.

Sydney had also produced *Armchair Theatre* for ABC, and a BBC version called *The Wednesday Play* came later. Both dealt with contemporary issues, such as drug addiction and teenage pregnancy. Regional dialects could be heard, rather than BBC English, and this was new. He had seen a lot of these social problems, growing up on the streets of Toronto where there were gamblers and con-men, winos, prostitutes and thieves. He knew a lot of their stories. From an early age, it became apparent that these people were very different to him. Sydney's individualism saw him carrying a pencil and a sketch pad, and when he first started out; he had a desire to sketch and paint people on the street in their natural environment. This later developed into an interest in film, when he replaced the pencil with the camera and aimed to inject this kind of realism into his films. There were characters out on the sidewalk whose traits and tales were ingrained in his own being, and he had an extraordinary talent for taking a concept or an idea and presenting it in a new way. Sydney could sometimes see things just out of the reach of ordinary everyday people, and this was evident in some of his work; the viewers felt like they were getting a glimpse of some future science or some real-life horror story happening out there right now.

Maurice Newman and his wife Bessie allowed their children enough space for their imaginations to flourish and grow. As a boy, Sydney loved to read and he soon realised stories based upon myths and magic were leaping out of fairy tales and philosophy books into the minds of writers and film-makers all the time. Inventions such as jet-engines, nuclear bombs, and microchips were still years away but, the new technologies of the last fifty years inspired writers such Jules Verne and more recently H. G. Wells. They dreamed up monsters and machines, and Sydney's generation became one of the first to be inspired by them. A boy with such interests could become quite a man if he gained an expertise and possessed a decent set of morals, and a strict Jewish upbringing made sure he towed the line.
Humans wandering about in time was nothing new but Sydney Newman is known now as a forward-thinker for many reasons,

including the appointment of, then secretary, Verity Lambert as the first producer of *Doctor Who*. For instance, Sydney wanted the characters to show their emotions – and he would not have understood these feelings unless he had felt them. He had stared into the void himself at points in his life and survived with a story or two to tell.

April Fool's Day 1917 was like any other day. The Union Flag hung high on Queen Street, a sprinkling of colour from the old empire in a sea of gloom. This was just before Prohibition struck Canada, which would mean, on top of dealing with the daily grind of poverty, war and malnutrition, that you could not even get a drink in a bar or a liquor store. Despite the horrors, Sydney grew up to love the hustle and bustle of Queen Street and the community he lived in. Since the end of the 19th century, Jewish immigrants had been coming into Toronto and settling in a district known as The Ward, and, of course, there had been trouble – anti-Semitic riots before Sydney was born. As a kid, he would watch men in dark flannels and flat caps or military personnel in different coloured uniforms as they walked down the street. Woman perambulated children but, on this April Fool's, there was not a great deal to laugh about. The scarcity of money meant people's stomachs rumbled during some of the most depressing days in history; whole countries were involved in the war, so hardship was inevitable. From the generals at the top, to the cobblers who mended the boots on the ground, it affected everyone. Freedom was at stake, and the world needed to be saved.

The family lived above a small shoe-shop that they owned, and it made just enough for them to survive. Sydney's daughter Jennifer later recalled that her father came from a traditional Jewish family, and his parents emigrated from Russia. (Spears, 1997) They were thankful for the trade in re-heeled jackboots and the end of the war was still 19 months away. Millions of men had already died in the muddy fields of France and Belgium in the name of the King; 16,000 more from the Canadian Expeditionary Force would be amongst the quarter of a million killed at Passchendaele by the end of the year, and for what? A few miles of mud which they eventually lost. Bessie Newman was in trouble also, her waters had broken and the general urgency of impending childbirth was under way, and Sydney was born on the kitchen table. (G. Newman[1], 2015)

Almost 5,000 soldiers and nurses did not return after the war. Slowly, people grieved for their dead as they rebuilt their lives, although the Great Depression hit first. During the 1920s, Toronto began gradually to prosper but, not all of its residents enjoyed the benefits. Working-class inhabitants continued to work long hours for low pay at places like Worts Distillery, Gooderham and the Gerhard Heintzman Piano Company, and they lived in inner-city slums such as Cabbagetown. The poorer neighbourhoods were characterised by dilapidated frame houses built at the end of the 19th century, when there were no minimum building standards and, although the Newman family were poor, they were not quite starving, even though there were two other children to feed. Sydney had an older sister called Ruth and a brother called Wilf. From an early age, Sydney was drawn to the USA; everybody wanted their own little piece of the American dream. It was regarded as the land of golden opportunities which was only reinforced when Hollywood movies came along and painted its idyllic pictures of how life could be. Having a creative mind, Sydney would have wanted to display his artwork, and later the films he made, and the place to do that was in LA.

Growing up around so many accents was quite an education, and most of the Canadian born kids, like him, spoke only English. Queen Street was a place where there was always something going on. Toronto was very different during the war and was largely undeveloped north of St Clair. At the turn of the century, the city numbered less than 250,000; by the end of the war the population had doubled. The Newmans were part of a larger Jewish community, but the city really was a melting pot of races and religions which did not always get on. Prostitute Corner had been established long before the 1920s, it was that sort of place. The ladies of the night would hide when the copper walked past and come back out after he had gone. Sydney's parents hated the place but, to him, it was home. There had always been a darker side to life on Queen Street. Murder, rape, and back-street abortions were not uncommon and a lot of it slipped under the radar, although the Metropolitan Police set up an abortion squad. Drinking and fornication were also sins, but, hell, it could be fun if you could get away with it.

Civil unrest was not uncommon in Canada, especially during the Depression. People were desperate and figured they had nothing to lose. In August 1918, Toronto experienced the biggest riot in its history, with the trouble aimed at Greek immigrants who were believed to be pro-German and not involved in the fighting during the war. It exploded after the expulsion of a crippled soldier from the White City Cafe by Greek waiters; the next day, 20,000 veterans destroyed every Greek business in the city centre and the Mayor had to call in the military. These were troubled times, but events never usually got as extreme. The worst Sydney and his friends saw, growing up, was policemen battling with crooks, or a knife or gun being pulled. After the Jewish migrants, many Italians started coming to the city in the 1920s, along with Scottish, English, Irish, and Finns to name but a few (Knowles, 2007).

There was always going to be trouble and if you were a keeper of the peace, you had to be able to look after yourself. It was helpful if you could keep a drunk upright with one hand whilst 'phoning for the Black Maria from the police callbox at the end of the street.

Chapter Two
Fairy Tales and Science Fiction

For five-year-old Sydney, books were essential reading, and favourites were written by H. G. Wells, Jules Verne, and Andrew Lang who wrote a whole series of fairy tales. Twelve were published between 1889 and 1910, each named after a colour. They contained a variety of tales rooted in ancient folklore and *The Lord of the Rings* author J. R. R. Tolkien was also influenced by them. They helped pave the way for the emerging genres of fantasy and science fiction. When Lang's first book, *The Blue Fairy Book*, was released, the public considered it too brutal for the children of the Empire – that sort of violence needed to be hidden away in places like the Boer concentration camps and Amritsar, not read aloud from the nursery rocking-chair. When it was published, authors such as Verne, C. I. Defontenay and Emile Souvestre already had science fiction on the newsstands and in bookshops; Lang's books popularised old myths and legends which were sometimes re-told using a futuristic or apocalyptic setting. Sydney absorbed them whilst attending Ogden Public School, which was a block north-east of Queen Street West and Spalding Avenue. (Bunch, 2013) Other than reading, the only academic subject he was interested in was art. He excelled at painting and drawing, and his talent would later spill into film.

From its inception, film has been able to glamourise and exaggerate reality. Whenever anybody tries to show drama that is close to the bone, there is usually a public outcry of some sort. Despite how desensitised we are today, modern film-makers are still producing hard-hitting documentaries and films. In Sydney's day, this was big news. The establishment was shocked, as were the viewers at home, when some of his *Armchair Theatre* plays tackled such themes head-on, and the term 'kitchen-sink drama' was coined. Stories such as *Look Back in Anger*, by John Osborne, and *Cathy Come Home*, by Jeremy Sandford, contained, for the first-time, issues about race, sexuality, teenagers and others on the edge of society in post-war Britain. This was Sydney at his best; he did not want to cater exclusively for the middle and upper-classes and he helped nurture and mould writers such as Alun Owen, Clive Exton, Harold Pinter and Dennis Potter.

Lang's fairy tales gave Sydney a fantasy world into which he could escape. He may well have scanned the rolling hills of Ontario for elves and unicorns living out there in the wilderness, or looked for a secret door in a hedgerow leading into the world of Lewis Carroll's Alice. When you consider popular fantasy and children's fiction in the first half of the 20th century, you see many precursors to later ideas and inventions. In C. S. Lewis's *The Lion, The Witch and The Wardrobe*, we see perhaps a template for the TARDIS time-machine, although Sydney was also impressed with H. G. Wells' book *The Time Machine*. Bigger within than without, the wardrobe in *The Lion, The Witch and The Wardrobe* is a portal between real life and the fantasy world of Narnia, and the notion of a large space contained within something smaller (like a police box) must be one of the greatest science fiction ideas of all-time. Even the Walt Disney film *Mary Poppins* (1964) got in on the act, with Mary's transcendental carpet bag.

It was only the concept for the TARDIS time-machine which Sydney brought to the table. Staff writer Anthony Coburn thought of using a police box, after Sydney said of the original proposal for the time-machine in C. E. Webber's notes from 1963: *"...something humdrum, say, passing through some common object in [the] street such as a night-watchman's shelter..."*

A police box was easy and cheap and Sydney wanted a symbol people would associate with the show, nobody could have imagined how iconic the TARDIS would become. It could be argued that it is as important a concept as the Daleks, and has certainly helped to sustain the show over the years when there was no appearance from Terry Nation's creation. Talk of moving through time and space at tea-time was a new idea, but would it wash with the great British public on a Saturday evening between the football scores and *The Telegoons*?

In the excellent TV dramatisation *Adventures in Time and Space*, about the early years of *Doctor Who*, Sydney is portrayed by actor Brian Cox as a loud-mouthed New Yorker. Sydney spoke with a softer Torontonian accent, although he could be just as energetic and enthusiastic as a stereotypical New Yorker. The character is not a true reflection of him. However, the story does show the viewer how enthusiastic he was, as well as the faith he had in other people.

There were many things which sparked Sydney's imagination, none more so than art and films. He looked destined to follow an artistic path through life from an early age and, as a teen, he was talented enough to think about art college. He had a good eye for detail as an artist, and as an aspiring creative-professional, but had no chance of getting any funding to take up the course. Things like that did not happen to poor kids in Canada. The Dominion-Provincial Student Loan Program, which began to create opportunities for people from low socio-economic groups to get some education, did not start operating until 1939. Back then, Sydney did not have a hope without some kind of sponsorship. After all, his father owned a perfectly good business, and people always needed shoes and boots re-heeled – and he would need someone to take over when he came to retirement, but it soon became apparent that it would not be Sydney, whose ideas were not so much above his station, just different to the rest of the world.

"I've always had goals, but I've always tried to try to sort of be aware of myself at that particular time to extend myself. When I was ten years old, I wanted to be a cartoonist, and when I was 13, 14, I wanted to be a painter, and when I was 19, I was a painter. And when I was 21, I didn't think I was a good enough painter and I became interested in film. Luckily, history intervened and the National Film Board came into existence, and I grabbed the opportunity and got a job!" (Newman[3], 1966)

Sydney was just another dreamer from Queen Street and a lot of what he saw inspired his work. He also knew how to talk to people, and the fact he was in touch with what was going on bled through into his work and gave it a new level of realism. He was not afraid to take a gamble and show the truth, whatever that may be. Throughout his professional career, Sydney would try out new ideas with varying degrees of success. The poverty the family lived in meant he never forgot his roots, and he was not the kind of man to let anybody walk over him. In the end, he did manage to get into Toronto Central Tech, but only on a commercial art course; even though there was a perception that doing so was a one-way ticket to poverty, it was what he loved. There was a world of difference between the penniless street artist hanging around on corners, selling the odd portrait to passers-by, and Sydney's vision of how it could be. There were art and design industries and opportunities opening that took full advantage of new technologies. Artists were needed to design and draw adverts, posters, and backdrops for magazines, films, and television programs but, of course, the family did not have the money to be frittered away on a whim, although Sydney really did understand the role of the artist on an emotional level.

He had also developed a useful sideline teaching art to children on Saturday mornings at the Toronto Gallery of Art. His chief, Arthur Lismer, asked him one day if he had ever shot a film. Newman said that he hadn't. "Well I want you to make one anyway," Lismer replied. He wanted a film of the children's activities at the art gallery and, to Newman's surprise, immediately borrowed a 16mm camera and handed it over saying, "You are a photographer and an artist." Newman recalls the movie with affection. "I thought it was the finest movie I ever made." (Greatorex, 1961)

So, it was Central Tech for me where, for four years, Carl Schaefer, Elizabeth Wynn Wood, Charlie Goldhammer and others suffered me somewhat gladly... And so, with a friend called Paul Petroff, I made my first film. (Newman[12], 1976)

Sydney had already started to develop an awareness of what people liked, and he was able to occasionally sell his work when he first started out. Later on, he would develop an audience awareness, and it became a skill he would grow to rely on as his career progressed, but he did not always get it right. As a young artist, he went to the movies as much as he possibly could. He got inspiration from films such as *Flash Gordon*, *The Return of Doctor X* and *Buck Rogers*, which were all smash-hits during the 1930s, and he sketched them all. As he grew older, he understood that he needed an idea that would blow people's minds, something from the worlds of H. G. Wells and Jules Verne rolled into one. The books he read and the films he watched started to change the way he looked at life, but the coming together of these ideas was still years away. With televisions beginning to appear in homes from the 1930s, people soon had access to a variety of programs. The first episode of *Doctor Who* was not shown until November 23,

1963, but the first proper science fiction serial went out in 1949. It was called *Captain Video and his Video Rangers* and it aired in the USA. It featured stories by famous writers such as Arthur C. Clarke, Isaac Asimov and Jack Vance. Shows such as *Tom Cobbett – Space Cadet*, *Space Patrol* and *Tales of Tomorrow* followed, and they all went out live. The origins of science fiction on TV can be traced back even further to the BBC, which broadcast a 35-minute extract from a play called *RUR* by Karel Čapek in 1938, which introduced the word 'robot' into the English language. There was also an adaption of H. G. Wells' *The Time Machine* in 1949, and the first British science fiction show arrived in 1951. It was called *Stranger from Space* and it starred future *Doctor Who* actor Valentine Dyall, who played the Black Guardian in four stories between 1979 and 1983.

Sydney soon started seeing the world as an artist, albeit a commercial one, and this would prove to be to his advantage as time went on and he began designing sets. Later on, he was able to look at scenes, acts and turning-points in a similar way, and he got to know what got under people's skins; many of the shows he produced had a strong focus on the human condition. It was not just the thrill-a-minute story-lines that appealed to him – he liked the idea of how people reacted in real-life situations, and it made good television. One of the observations he made was the close link between humour and fear. Actors such as Harold Lloyd and Charlie Chaplin used such techniques to great effect before the talkies took over, and if it worked for them, it could work for Sydney.

After leaving college, Sydney discovered for himself the romantic notion of the struggling artist was not all it was cracked up to be. He was not bringing in enough money to put food on the table or light the fire now that he had left home, and Canadian winters could be long and cold. The fact that he did not have two coins to rub together meant that he stood very little chance of buying luxuries, or taking a girl out if he could find the right one – and he did have offers. He felt he was swimming against the tide at that point in his life and this may have led him out of the creative industry altogether to spend his life in a factory or shop. There were no markers flagging him up as anything special and, at that time, everyone wanted to be an artist or a movie star. Who, in their right mind, wanted to spend their life down the pit, or in a mill or factory?

There were people that you would have picked out as great, and others you would have laughed at; Sydney sat between the two. A spark was needed to get everything coming together, although he was never short of ideas. In his heart, he thought he might come up with something if he kept on trying. It would take a combination of talent, ingenuity, good luck, and bullshit, but he knew he could mix it with the best of them if he could somehow get a chance to prove his worth. Things had been tough for the Newman family, and Sydney was not the most affluent student at the college but he was certainly one of the most resilient, which turned out to be a good skill because he did not have a lot going for him at the time other than a head full of dreams about comic-book heroes and rocket-ships.

By doing odd jobs, and by picking up the odd commercial assignment, Sydney just about made enough to exist when he left college, and he soon started to wonder what else there was that he could do. A host of ideas and influences were stewing in his mind – the art, surrealism, and the science fiction were all helping him to develop. The world geared up for another conflict and, in his book The Shape of Things to Come, H. G. Wells predicted the Second World War six years before it started. Writers such as Aldous Huxley and George Orwell published novels before and after the conflict which prophesied such things as a new world order, test-tube babies and CCTV. Writers and scientists had a good idea of what the future held but the world had to deal with the Nazi war machine first. An alarming rise in anti-Semitism was spreading through Germany and Europe and news filtered back to the Jewish communities in Canada. It looked bleak; some were even coming to Toronto and taking their positions in the queues for food and water.

Sydney had a moral duty to serve his country, but this did not stop his stomach rumbling. There was always the Navy or the Army, and, in the end, he did his bit for the war effort although in his hand was a camera, rather than a rifle.

On September 10, 1939, just a week after Great Britain declared war on Germany, Canada joined the fight. It must have been strange for 22-year-old Sydney as he looked out across Lake Ontario to see the twinkling lights of Wilson, USA – a body of water was all that separated a warring nation from one still at peace. Most Americans saw Europe as a mess. They also viewed the First World War as a mistake and they did not want to get involved, until Japan forced their hand at Pearl Harbour. A week after joining the war, the Royal Canadian Navy was escorting their first transatlantic convoys; two weeks after that, facilities were set up to train pilots from Britain and the rest of the Commonwealth. By now, Sydney realised the power of taking real-life situations and using them on the stage and screen. What he later looked for from a script was a plot that created an understanding of the characters and their situation – how they reacted – which made good drama. He was just like the artist at the easel ready to paint from instinct; his feelings and state of mind as the brush touches the canvas are his guide. All the pain, all the preconceptions of society and psychology powering him through, produced the kind of passion which made Sydney tick as an artist, and, later, as a producer. Love, hate, sex, death, fear, loneliness, isolation and elation were the colours in the pallet; a skilful writer or director would craft into words or scenes the same feelings as the painter.

Despite the terrible deeds and atrocities of the Second World War, creativity flourished in art, as well as drama; everybody hoped and prayed for a better future. Influences came from science and technology, and inventions and ideas were thought up by men like Albert Einstein, Robert Oppenheimer, Tommy Flowers, Frank Whittle and Wernher von Braun. Books and films asked the question on everyone's minds: why had the war happened? People saw the horrors on the newsreels as it unfolded but it stopped nobody in their tracks. Film-making could be a risky business, too, but some mad fools had to do it. At least the soldiers had guns. After the war, it took time for people to understand the atrocities that had been committed and the full scale of death and destruction. By the 1960s, liberty and freedom for all was what the majority wanted, as well as their own piece of the American dream, of course. Still the conflicts rumbled on, in Vietnam, Israel, and Pakistan, to name but a few. During the war, a steady influx of poor immigrants had become a problem, and this did not stop as soon as peace came. On streets all over the world, there were starving toddlers and babies; elderly people huddled around fires trying to keep warm, wondering if they would return to Vienna, Warsaw, Berlin, and Amsterdam, and young helping old and sharing their bread. This could be seen right outside the Newman family home on Queen Street. People had fled across land and sea to escape the Nazis, and, later, many would recall their tales of woe.

Chapter Three
Taking Money From the Commies

The central idea behind *Doctor Who*, that of a doddery old man and his granddaughter running away and having great adventures, was not a new idea. It had been explored in books, films and plays. William Hartnell's cranky Doctor character was the crazy genius lost in time and space, just like those old men on the streets of Toronto Sydney had seen during the dark old days. Many had been doctors and professors back home, but now they were lost and they had to hold out their hands for food and water like everybody else. Titles meant nothing on the street and if they were lucky, they would not be alone – a child or a grandchild would be there for company and support; a terrible state of affairs to face in old age. In *Doctor Who*, Carole Ann Ford fulfilled a similar role. In her early 20s in 1963, Carole Ann played super-intelligent Susan Foreman, the "Unearthly Child". Sydney did not want her to be the Doctor's granddaughter; he wanted their situation to create mystery – why would a young girl be travelling with the Doctor if they were not related? What had happened to them and why had the mysterious old man lost his memory? Her story-arc evolves from a frightened teen from another world into an independent woman who falls in love with David Campbell in *The Dalek Invasion of Earth*, and many fans of the modern show have called for a reunion between the Doctor and Susan. Teen viewers were supposed to identify because of her youthful innocence and teen angst, and she shared an alien aloofness with her aged scientist grandfather. Sydney's specification was that she needed to be able to scream.

Anthony Coburn's cavemen tale was not the original storyline for the show, but it ended up kicking off the whole franchise after teachers Ian Chesterton and Barbara Wright stumble into a junkyard in London, and then into the TARDIS itself, in pursuit of their mysterious pupil Susan Foreman. Originally scheduled as the second story of the series, with C. E. Webber's *Nothing at the End of the Lane / The Giants* as the first until Sydney told him he was not happy with the story and noted that it was "thin on incident and character" and overambitious when considered in light of the budget. The use of large-scale sets and visual effects was not practical, and interim producer Rex Tucker was in agreement – it would also be impossible to make it at Lime Grove Studio D where 24 *Doctor Who* stories were filmed between 1963 and 1972. After Sydney rejected the scripts, Coburn was asked to re-write *An Unearthly Child* so it could open the show. Themes and ideas from *The Giants* were later incorporated into the season two story *Planet of the Giants*, but Louis Marks' tale was different; it took up more of an environmental theme and was less pacy.

Doctor Who happened to be the right idea at the right time, although you would not have guessed it in the beginning, and Sydney would be eternally grateful for its success.

The idea smashed together the work of Lang, Wells, Verne and Orwell to create characters who could travel through time and space in a police box. The show has developed considerably over the years, which is a credit to the strength of the original idea. Without those alterations and revisions, it would not have lasted for as long as it did, and Sydney understood that as the years passed by. He did not always agree with the direction it took, and, by then, he had nothing to do with the show. He was never hands-on like Gene Roddenberry, the creator of *Star Trek* who wrote and produced episodes, books, and scripts. Once *Doctor Who* was set up, Sydney stepped away and left it to his producer, Verity Lambert, to make it a reality, and he was never acknowledged in the credits at the end of show.

To be confident in his characters and their situations, Sydney needed to understand them inside out. He knew that making the balance between their feelings and emotions and the situation a precarious one would work, because of what he had learned about audiences. Fans of the show make the comparison between the Daleks, created by Welsh television writer Terry Nation, and the Nazis. In *Genesis of the Daleks* (1975), the similarities between their Kaled forefathers and the SS is uncanny and the characters of the Doctor and his granddaughter have their roots in the same conflict. The people Sydney saw waiting in line for bread as a boy appeared in the Communist posters he would design, and, later, in some of his shows. They were trying to survive as unwanted aliens but, in Toronto, they were equal in their nothingness – so many classes and dialects, a melting pot of human beings defined by the boundary lines of the kingdoms on their maps.

Like all youngsters, he was trying out his new freedom, and meeting new people, and it was then he was given the chance to design posters for the Canadian Communist Party. When the organisation began in 1921, it was an illegal operation and, in 1931, eight of its leaders were imprisoned for advocating the use of violence to overthrow the government. During its existence, the party drifted from legal to illegal and back again, but, to Sydney, the posters were just a way to earn a little more money and meet new people. Admittedly, he could have found an organisation less controversial to work for, but being in the precarious financial position he was in, he could not afford to say no, and it is fair to say he did see the common-sense in some of the Communist ideals. He also knew how rare jobs were, especially in the entertainment industry – it had been that way since the stock market crashed in 1929 – and he needed to make a living. He did not want to return home with his tale between his legs; he wanted to carve his own groove. It would have been difficult to define himself as a film-maker back then but he was certainly an artist, and he was regarded as one of Toronto's best graphic designers by the end of the 1930s. If you were earning a wage, you were lucky; by 1933, 30 percent of the people in Toronto were unemployed – although there were some opportunities in construction, with many Torontonian landmarks being erected at this time – so what harm could it do to make a few dollars from designing posters for the commies?

Soon, Sydney was hard at work, designing covers for magazines and for Russian films that were shown in Canada, but there is no record of him ever joining the party, and he is credited only for his poster work. Deep down, he was not passionate enough about the cause. In 1936, some 1,200 of their most fanatical supporters travelled to Spain to help fight Franco's fascist movement which was sweeping through the country and, although he was not involved, his involvement with the party would come back to haunt him.

Because of Sydney's love for film and performance, along with his ability to paint a good backdrop, he also became involved with a short-lived movement called *The Theatre of Action*. Among their ranks were Lorne Green (of *Bonanza* fame) and Sydney Banks, and reviews described them as a left-wing drama company. Sydney's involvement was another step-up in his career, and certainly a moment of significant personal development as he began to move away from the more traditional roles of the artist, like sketching and painting, to designing sets and then later becoming involved in production and direction. Records at the University of Guelph in Ontario show that he designed the set for Milo Hastings and Orrie Lashin's *Class of '29*, in 1937, and *Steel* – both directed by David Pressman. He did all the design with his friend Nathan Cohen, and the group won awards at the Dominion Drama Festival which ran between 1932 and 1978.

During the Depression, the Festival kept the candle burning for Canadian talent and produced new plays throughout those dark years. Communism was starting to be seen in a far less favourable way leading up to the Second World War, and some of the themes that *The Theatre of Action* were putting into their plays was not for the palate of the festival organisers, who saw them as Communist sympathisers and possible supporters of the Nazi Party. Perhaps Sydney sensed this, or it could have been that opportunities were starting to open up for him elsewhere? Whatever the reason, he was not involved for long, but he did make some great contacts and friends. One of them was composer Louis Applebaum, who went on to score music for hundreds of films and received a nomination for an Academy Award for *The Story of G.I. Joe*. There was also Torontonian Sydney Banks, who had been a child actor in England before becoming the first television producer in Canada when the television service got underway. With such creative types around him, Sydney was starting to learn and develop some fantastic skills and talents, like his ability to be introspective, and to draw out of his characters something that was believable and real. If it was anger or joy, even if it broke the hearts of the audience, it was a winner, and Sydney's approach as a producer was far more artistic, than executive, although he acquired those skills as his career progressed and he ended up in more senior positions. The war would bring him an even bigger opportunity but, before that, he thought his ship had come in and an opportunity arose at the Walt Disney Company in America as a graphic designer. In the end, he would be denied a visa and that was the end of it, and film-making came calling once again. At the end of the war, he would be given the opportunity to direct his own films and he became an integral part of the National Film Board of Canada, but the transition from artist and set-designer took a little while.

Hollywood, where the streets are paved with gold and everyone knows a movie star, or a director – at least, that is what Sydney believed when he arrived in California. In the 1920s, Paramount, Warner Bros, RKO, and Columbia set up their studios and the place became one of the biggest industries in America overnight. The nickname 'Tinseltown' was coined because of the glitzy image of the movie industry and the glamorous premieres the studios put on. Film stars have walked down the red carpet into the cities' movie theatres for generations and, if you want to make it as a star, this is the place to conquer. Everyone wants to be that one in a million and, for the wannabes, it is tough, really tough. In 1938, James Cagney's *Angels with Dirty Faces* and *The Wizard of Oz*, with Judy Garland, were in production. There was a buzz around the place when all of this was happening, and being close to it was exciting and frustrating in equal measures for Sydney. He quickly learnt the difference between the cinematographic world of fantasy and illusion, and the real one in which his stomach rumbled and it did not take him long to see that this was not a land of opportunity for an unskilled kid. During the early part of the 1930s, the movie business had boomed; by the middle of the decade, the Depression had hit even Hollywood; the studios were in the middle of a publicity drive to recapture lost audiences, and nobody was hiring.

The dream shattered quickly for Sydney, although he was offered the job with Disney as an animator and he was overjoyed. Still his enthusiasm and determination remained relentless despite the knock-backs he had already taken, and this one was destined to fall through, too. Nevertheless, it helped him to develop a logical determination and a never-say-die attitude that stayed with him for life, which sounded very much like the basis of a strong character on the screen: a tale about an alien new to England like he would become, perhaps? How much of the initial concept for Doctor Who was self-reflective? He was pretty much an unknown when he first arrived in England, except to the British television people, who were largely unconcerned about him in the beginning. With skills from artist to film-maker, he was, early on, a jack-of-all-trades who possessed a rugged determination. Maybe there was more of Sydney in the character of the Doctor than he has been given credit for in the past? He always tried to do the right thing, and was never fazed by failure and rejection – beliefs and ideas which ran through both the man and the fictional character: never giving up on the hope of discovering new ideas, or different ways of looking at a problem; waiting patiently for the moment and it would come. Sydney was sure of it; was certain of it. He would bloody well make it happen, else. There was no turning back after all the effort and heartache, but still there was a problem. The Disney job did not work out because he was ultimately denied a visa. Any attempts to try again would have quickly been scuppered because, at the beginning of the Second World War, anyone of conscription age who escaped to the USA was quickly labelled a coward.

Chapter Four
A Fight for Freedom and Freewill

From its earliest days to the new series of *Doctor Who* (which started in 2005), a common theme runs through both: adventures where the Doctor and his companions become involved with an oppressed people fighting a common aggressor. We see this developing as early on as the second story, *The Daleks* (1963), where the time-travellers risk their lives and team up with the Thals in their struggle for survival. Such tales often show a desperate clash of ideologies, and free will and betrayal are overarching themes; Sydney was well read on such issues, and he liked his writers to try to examine the inner workings of the mind in their work, rather than simply showing brutality or acts of love without reason. In *The Dalek Invasion of Earth* (1964), robotised-humans with little or no capacity for free thought are controlled by the Daleks through headsets, but they soon break down as their brains rebel, and they commit suicide. This implies some sort of self-awareness or, at least, a moment of clarity. Never mind what Sydney initially thought of the motorised-dustbins, these were the sorts of ideas good science fiction should be throwing out there at the dawn of the space-age.

Ideas about freewill take us into the realms of psychiatry and philosophy but, once Sydney had accepted the idea of the Daleks, he would have been excited by the big issues that writer Terry Nation tackled in his scripts, such as genocide and genetics; it was right up his alleyway, so to speak. Stories about an oppressed alien race are a great way to tell a tale about an Earthly injustice, and a very powerful tool. The noble idea of the fight for survival and the protection of all you have, including your history, meant a lot to Sydney, and it helped him to shape his own internal narrative, and the way stories and ideas played out in his head. Examples of characters that operated close-to-the-bone in immediate life-or-death situations are scattered throughout his work, and, if you got the actors and the story right, he knew real-life situations made great television. *Doctor Who* sometimes struggled to make shows look real, with wooden acting, as well as sets. His involvement with the show was not as hands-on – he had been employed as a producer on earlier productions such as *Armchair Theatre*, which brought him closer to the work. He could still insist on changes, but Verity Lambert was in charge and she did well considering there was neither the time nor the money to develop characters, effects, and scenarios. Consequently, the quality of shows varied. Some scripts looked fantastic on paper and became a living nightmare to produce; others slipped from the hands of the editors rather quietly and did big things. It all depended on chemistry – if that was there between actors, supporting actors, and the crew, and the script was okay, the show could be great. It either happened naturally, or the whole production was mundane, which meant the show suffered and appeared amateur or farcical at times.

Sydney would have recognised the revolutionary impulse the Doctor and his companions instil in the Thals in Terry Nation's first story *The Daleks* in 1963, but not until it had become a phenomenal success! Issues that were on people's minds at the time – those of nuclear devastation, genetic mutation, and the struggle for life after the bomb has been dropped – were also addressed and, without this story, *Doctor Who* would have almost certainly ended within a few years. The Daleks are, of course, a meld of machine and flesh, rather than bug-eyed monsters. Inside their casings sit genetically modified creatures. They are ruthless and robot-like in their manner and this frightened people when they first saw or heard one speak. Part of their appeal was the fact that children were able to imitate them in the playground, which helped their popularity grow, yet nobody would have guessed the Daleks would create a stir comparable to Beatlemania in Britain for a while. Very soon you could buy Rolykins Dalek toys and Lincoln Anti-Dalek guns as their renown spread out across the world. There was even a single by The Go-Go's, called *I'm Gonna Spend my Christmas with a Dalek*, which was released at the end of 1964.

The show's success was astronomical and it would have been easy for Sydney to have taken more credit if he had been that way inclined and barged his way in once it was a hit. He, though, knew it was Verity's baby; his role was as overseer and creator, and the man at whose feet the blame would fall if it failed or if the use of a mysterious man in a time-travelling box had scared the kids too much, like it did before for this was not the first time he had made a show like this. (See details about *Howdy Doody* in chapter 9). In time, he moved away and became disappointed with *Doctor Who* later in life but he was always proud of its success. When it started, everyone was running flat out to make it work. What it may have lacked in time and budget, it made up for in other ways – it left a lasting effect on the imagination. People read science fiction when they were children and were blown away by the 'what ifs?' When you are young, anything is possible, even aliens on other planets or a cloak of invisibility. Television and film were bringing these ideas to life on screen and, on many occasions, *Doctor Who* did this rather well; with big prime-time audiences, it slipped into the public consciousness almost overnight and, thus, the foundation stone was laid for the brand it has become today. When William Hartnell was replaced as the Doctor by Patrick Troughton in 1966, the BBC knew the show and the Daleks were popular enough to continue with a new lead, just as companions had come and gone in the past. Through the process of regeneration, new Doctors, companions, and production teams have been used, and the show has rebooted and rebranded a number of times.

The transmission of the first episode of *An Unearthly Child* on November 23, 1963, was overshadowed by the events that occurred in Dallas the day before, when US President John F. Kennedy was assassinated. That was all people thought of, and the show may have sunk without a trace had it not been for the Daleks story. It aired five weeks later and the end of episode one will always be remembered for rocketing the show towards the phenomenal success it is. It is the scene where Jacqueline Hill's character, Barbara Wright, is pinned against the wall as a Dalek's sucker bares down. The look of terror on her face, her wild staring eyes as it probes ever nearer for the cliff-hanger, is reminiscent of the best Hammer Horror and Alfred Hitchcock films. It was television and *Doctor Who* at its best, and, boy, it was scary for Saturday tea-time viewing. The Daleks became hot stuff, but the longevity of the show cannot be put down to their appearances alone although every expert acknowledges their importance. Lots of other elements make up the show's mythology, and this has helped it to evolve, but Sydney's basic premise of a man in a box travelling through time and space is still in place.

Sydney realised early that opportunities rarely came to your door and he would have to go out and get what he wanted, but his was not a ruthless determination. He was modest and honest, and called a spade a spade. He knew how to voice his opinion without being outspoken but, in the BBC in the early 1960s, the 'American' accent alone was enough to label him a loudmouth. A maverick and an outsider he may have been but the Corporation desperately needed somebody with a new take on things, and he knew how the best television worked in Canada and the USA before he came to England. With a degree of charm underpinning his expertise, he was still able to work well with almost everyone, and there would not have been many who secretly disliked him, or the way he went about things, come the end of his time in England. He would go on to change the way BBC Drama did things forever, and he helped the Corporation realise they needed to compete with the hugely popular ITV, which had started seven years before his arrival. He had held the same position at ABC and he made his bosses acknowledge the impact of commercial television. Until then, the BBC adopted a rather snobby attitude towards their programs as being of superior quality; they were not interested until ITV shows were all over the newspapers and people were talking about them in the street. Sydney Newman was going to be the man who would ride into the BBC on his horse, wearing his ten-gallon hat, and change the face of British television forever - that was the attitude of the old guard. He certainly did the last part.

What Sydney may have lacked academically, he more than made up for in commonsense and knowledge – not every genius is testable under exam conditions. You cannot scrutinise, with academic or mathematical certainty, the strokes of an artist's brush or the way an actor rouses the audience at the start of a play. As the Second World War rumbled on, Sydney was steadily making progress and meeting the right kinds of people. He got another break after leaving Central Tech in Toronto when his caricatures of Canadian businessmen ran in the *Financial Post*. He also managed to sell some of his photos to *Saturday Night Magazine*, whilst he was also designing sets for amateur productions, and it was then that the newly-formed National Film Board of Canada became of interest to him. With his love for cinema, he was well aware of the *Canada Carries On* newsreels and theatrical shorts which they started making in 1940. Designed as propaganda and to boost morale, Londoner Stuart Legg went on to win the NFB its first Oscar in 1942 with *Churchill's Island*, with another of his films - *War Clouds Over the Pacific* – also being nominated. Legg was also part of a group of British film-makers called The Documentary Film Movement, which was fronted by the legendary film-maker John Grierson who became the first commissioner of the NFB when it grew out of the National Film Commission.

Born in Stirling in 1898, John Grierson is known as the father of documentary films; he even coined the name 'documentary' in a review he was writing. He argued that real-life situations captured on film are, in themselves, an art-form, and that 'original' actors and scenes are better than their fictional counterparts. Some of his films showed the struggle people faced during the Depression, or in times of disaster and war. By his own admission, Sydney learned a lot from Grierson, and we can certainly see where his passion for realism came from. If he could make fiction like real-life, then surely it would feel closer to home to people than some of the terrible movies and awful adaptations of classic literature they showed on the BBC. How about showing to the viewer characters and situations like the ones they saw in the street, or down at the shops, or heard about in the pub? He would have to master the art of documentary-making first, though, but he was extremely lucky to fall under the wing of Grierson; there could not be a finer teacher.

"Grierson was to become a unique individual in the world of film in that he was not a film-maker, having directed only one film, the classic Drifters *(1929) which depicted the work of Scottish fishermen. Not for him was the time-consuming, patient process of writing, photography, direction and editing. Rather, knowing how to do it, and recognising how it should be done, he became a producer, but a producer the like of which had never been seen before and has never been seen since.*

"Part artist, part impresario, part instructor, part mentor, he had the vision to see what should be done and how it should be done, and he inspired others into doing it, not necessarily in his fashion, but in their own terms, invigorated by his intense beliefs and enthusiasm. Grierson was shabbily treated by the Canadian government as a result of the Gouzenko spy trials. He was barred from taking an important position at the UN, and returned to England a discouraged man." (Pratley, 1982)

Chapter Five
Life at the NFB

"I was a very successful commercial artist at the time, sometimes earning as much as a hundred dollars a week, and I gave it all up to earn a hundred dollars a month at the Film Board. It didn't matter, the money was unimportant, and I became a film-maker. In my ten years at the film-board, I guess I was associated with about 350 films. I started as a splicer-boy and learned how to handle the stuff, and I wrote many of the films, and I eventually became producer, then executive producer and I got interested in the educational aspects of film-making – the information aspects – and therefore became fascinated in television." (Newman[3], 1966)

Not wanting to appear a draft dodger, Sydney did not pursue the visa and the job at Disney much to his disappointed, and he missed a golden era for the company. During the Second World War, they made *Pinocchio, Fantasia, Dumbo* and *Bambi*, as well as training and propaganda films for every branch of the US military. The government looked at Walt Disney to do his bit for the war effort and to build the morale of the people. By 1942, most employees were off fighting, and Disney made war-related films which featured the studio's characters; *Der Fuehrer's Face* won an Academy Award for best short movie the following year. In 1941, the Molotov Ribbentrop Pact ended; the Nazis invaded the Soviet forces in Eastern Poland; and Sydney was glad he had broken all ties with the Reds long before. It was then that he got a job with the NFB as a production assistant which was another step up for him, professionally. It also meant he would need to up his game and focus, sometimes like he was organising a military campaign himself, although this was not always the work-ethic and such structure could restrict creativity. He would take a risk, and did so throughout his career, and could have easily destroyed his reputation, but he succeeded more times than he failed.

"In any institution, there has to be leadership, and there has to be people who are burgeoning out, and whose enthusiasm and creative abilities are at an exciting stage of flowering...

There should be more people who have grown up into the administrative levels, who have grown-up through the actual creative process itself, because, let's face it, creative people are the most difficult citizens of any community. It's part of their role to be iconoclastic in a sense, and part of their role in a society to prick our consciousnesses as ordinary people, and I think, in recognising of what a healthy community is compounded, we have to support these 'nutty kooks' who lead." (Newman[3], 1966)

Sydney's gambles were not those of a meticulous planner whose objective was always to remain in control. There was looseness to his approach, a relaxed attitude which could be maintained only by not worrying about what would happen the next day. He also knew how to work right on the edge of what was acceptable to the viewer, and some of his best work came from this position. All that time he had spent in the cinema, he learned from the audience, too. He could picture in his mind their reaction to a scene throughout his life, and this gift is what made him such a good film-maker.

Many things worked differently during the war and, unless you had a reserved occupation, there was always the chance of being called up to fight. Actors, sports stars, painters and singers all did their duty and, in Britain, performances and events were limited because of the black-out and travel restrictions. *Doctor Who* founder and pioneer, co-creator Donald Wilson, served with the 43rd (Wessex) Infantry Division during the conflict, whilst the first Doctor, William Hartnell, served in the Tank Corps until he was invalided out.

From Nazi-looking guards to a Dalek in *The Dalek Invasion of Earth* shouting 'The final solution', we can see that the wartime experiences of many writers and directors were incorporated into the show's stories. It is also interesting to note that there was no story set in the Second World War during those early years, although a story called *The Nazis,* to be written by Brian Hayles, was planned before *The Smugglers* was developed instead. Also *Operation Werewolf,* set during D-day, written by Douglas Camfield and Robert Kitts was submitted in 1967 but was abandoned when producer Innes Lloyd left. The producers and directors were trying to look towards the future with stories like *The Daleks* and *The Sensorites,* and to the distant past with *Marco Polo* and *The Reign of Terror.* Whether Sydney would have allowed the Doctor to meddle in recent history such as D-Day or Dieppe at that time is unknown but many great war films had already been made so, if it was a good strong story and they could make it look real, it may have stood a chance. It is interesting to note that the only *Doctor Who* story from the original series set in the war was The Curse of Fenric in 1989, so there was certainly no rush for the Doctor to have an adventure in the Second World War.

Turning the Motion Picture Bureau into the National Film Board, John Grierson made sweeping changes, but his war-time message had to be blasted out to the masses, and Sydney had to start at the bottom of the ladder. He knew a good thing when he came across it, though, and Grierson's reputation alone would have been enough to convince him he was making the right move and would really enhance his learning. After all the false starts he had had in Hollywood, he was smart enough to realise he had at last got a foot in the door of the movie industry. Okay, it was not Disney or MGM, but being taken under the wing by a motion picture-maker like John Grierson turned a young creative Canadian (who was not quite sure where his true talent was) into a film-maker. What he learned from him, and how he put his own slant upon that knowledge, was what made him become the powerhouse who became known, not just in Canada and Britain, but throughout the world.

In 1940, people could get their news only from newspapers, radios, and cinema newsreels, and the NFB was faced with the challenge of making propaganda films to help with the war effort. This was the basis of the series *Canada Carries On* and of *World in Action*, which was also made by the NFB. Grierson and his crew wanted films that were hard-hitting and well distributed, and this is when Sydney really began to start cutting his teeth in the business. Grierson worked with the Wartime Information Board in Canada, and the aim of the films was to show Canada's achievements at home and abroad. The first one was produced and directed by Stuart Legg in 1940 and called *Atlantic Patrol*. Narrated by Lorne Green, it was black and white and lasted for ten minutes. It was not until 1943 that Sydney got the chance to direct one himself. *Fighting Norway* also ran for ten minutes, and it showed the collaboration of Canada and Norway in the war, and the vital role of the Norwegian underground. Before this, Sydney produced *Banshees Over Canada*, which looked at how Britain dealt with the Blitz in preparation of Canada ever facing such terror. There were, of course, strict restrictions on what the NFB could show, and what they could not, and it was not until these were relaxed after the war that Sydney and the other film-makers started to think more freely. Out of the destruction, stories were emerging of acts of bravery, as well as the atrocities committed by some. By the end of the war, it could be said that Sydney knew his craft well; he knew how to use the camera, and had an idea of the kinds of messages he wanted to put out there:

"Whilst we do not forget the responsibility inherent in the Film Board being a publicly-owned creative institution, we would be remiss if not taking advantage of the fact that it is not judged by its financial profitability. Through the freedom and self-expression it provides its film-makers, it helps foster a healthy self-awareness in the country.

I felt it was important today to try to relate some of the activities to the broad objective of the Film Board – helping Canadians use the media instead of being used by them, so we can better understand ourselves as individuals, our sovereign country, and the problems we face." (Newman[1])

It took a while for him to make what he would have called a good documentary, and he would later discover that making television drama appear realistic was an equally tricky task. The term 'kitchen-sink realism' sums up an earthy quality that is evidence in stories about everyday people forced into dire situations that the establishment is reluctant to acknowledge. Subjects such as drug addiction and teen pregnancy featured in plays and they had a shock value. The phrase was coined in the 1950s and knocked the fairy-dust off the problems portrayed by TV to reveal the grime, dirt and working class problems of the city below. This type of drama exposed the morals and the raw emotions of people caught in these situations, and Sydney would always try to capture this; it was one of his main aims as a director, and then a producer, although he did not always succeed. He also realised that this could be found in fantastical situations, too, and this is why his work crossed the genres so effectively – he always tried to give it an edge. It is hard to define the way he made drama, but he liked it to pull on the heart-strings and people needed to be able to relate to some of the problems because they had been through it themselves. At times, *Doctor Who* struck a good balance between realism and fantasy and those would have been the stories Sydney was happiest with when he originally saw the scripts, although he did concede to the tipping of the balance towards fantasy and scary monsters made from latex and foam when he saw the ratings and publicity.

"The fact is, in human drama, the relationships between – what are we talking about? – say a priest and a worshipper, or a boss and an employee, or a child and a father. I mean, these are the sort of eternal elements that are inherent in all drama. The terms by which you express it can change stylistically...

We try to do these plays about the turning-points in a country. What are the points of change? England, of course, is a terribly dramatic country since the war because of the growing realisation of the new, and changed, and reduced, status in the world. Its effect on the population in dozens of ways, and all this stuff, is the stuff of drama... The writers are inspired by it, and this is what we do...
These plays weren't sordid, or sexy, or filled with dirt, doubt, and disbelief, which is a phase. They were plays really about the working-class, and, for the first time in England, the working-class was being presented not as comic-foil. This paid

off in enormous amounts of profit for my employers at ABC Television, but it somehow fitted in with the commercial television operation of selling items worth thruppence and three shillings. Cheap little items that were bought like soap, bought by millions. And here were plays that were expressive to them, and so they flocked to commercial television." (Newman[3], 1966)

Starting out as a documentary-maker with the man who invented the word was not a bad beginning, and the films Sydney was making were getting better as he developed an eye for the grey area between reality and fiction, where some of his best programmes sat. It was difficult to always strike this balance with *Doctor Who*, and understanding this way of thinking gives us an insight into how he wanted it done. He desired people to believe and be educated but, most of the time, they were too busy being frightened out of their wits by Daleks or Voord. Of course, it had to be realistic to a degree, and having a schoolmaster, and a schoolmistress to counterbalance William Hartnell's cantankerous Doctor was good thinking. They were able to see the alien worlds they visited from the perspective of ordinary everyday people, and the subjects they taught were science and history. The idea was that, one week, the show would be set in the future and, the next, it would be set in the past. Everything would be nicely balanced, with the never-ending mystery coming from that element of unknown. Who was the Doctor, and where would his endless wanderings take him? That question is still being asked more than 50 years later. In those early years, there was not so much emphasis placed upon who the Doctor was – the characters were too busy getting out of situations, and Sydney's brief for the series implies there should always be mystery surrounding him. In the 2005 re-boot of the show, some of that mystery has been eroded and it could be argued that a little too much of the Doctor has been revealed, which was not the way Sydney originally saw him.

Sydney was not reckless; he took calculated risks, but he could not have predicted what his move to Britain would do to Canadian television, and he would one day return to help revive it. What was his magic formula? It is hard to pin down, but watching and listening to him in archive material shows how relaxed he was and he created an environment in which creativity could flourish, and he kept the bureaucrats at bay so they could produce and direct new shows. Was Sydney anti-establishment? In some ways he was, but there was also an ambition to reform television drama into broader, more down-to-earth, viewing for the everyday person, rather than topple the empire. He liked to make programmes about ordinary people in extraordinary situations so he had to take risks, and he did not worry about his job if it all went wrong. If he took a gamble, you could be sure he had done his research before he rolled the dice. Living on their nerves was how the crew survived when there was no way of recording shows and all television went out live. When you work this way, you became conditioned like a Pavlovian dog reacting to a bell, and Sydney took these skills with him when he moved to the BBC. If he failed, well, what the hell? He would just move on to the next job and make it a success. Some you win, some you lose.

Sydney liked to ask questions about the here and now, as well as about events from the past, so he could consider their consequences for the future. What would be the fate of mankind? Where was his progress taking him and what would be the expense? If the Earth would die one day and humanity would be destroyed, what did anything matter anyway? Who really gave a hoot, and who said the voice of authority was always right? Art had to push the boundaries, but how far should it go? It was something Sydney spent many hours pondering. As a film-maker, what could he do with his skills and power? How could he put across a message to the viewer that did not forecast doom and gloom? Like Grierson, his job was to recognise talent that could answer some of these questions or, at the very least, have a go at explaining some of the mysteries which made up life's rich tapestry – notions of good and evil, sex and love, war and death, as well as money and the consequences of having none could be explored just as well in a bed-sit in Liverpool as they could in some city in the future.

Chapter Six
War Films

When Sydney arrived at the National Film Board in 1941, the *Canada Carries On* series of predominantly 20-minute features were being shown in around 800 movie theatres every six months, and were distributed by Columbia Pictures. Grierson had extraordinary power over the way Canadians perceived the war, and his was a massive responsibility. He was able to import the talent that he wanted, which included some of the best producers, directors, animators and musicians in the world. A number of Britons were working for him and, without the war, it is highly unlikely that he would have been able to put together such a collective, with the likes of Disney and MGM sniffing around and paying good money. The NFB was, however, a place where some of the greats cut their teeth in the industry, and they won their fair share of the highest accolades, too. Today, they remain a bedrock of Canadian culture which Sydney tried to embrace in his work as much as he possibly could.

In Britain, hell rained from the skies. Some of the films that the NFB made told of this struggle, and they continued to do so after the war ended. There were tough rules and restrictions on the other side of the Atlantic and rationing would continue until July 1954. Cities and communities were destroyed in a darkness illuminated only by fire spilling out of houses and shops. When the hell finally ended, the rebuild would begin. All the while, America shined bright, lit by neon, and many people in Britain began to look through Hollywood-tinted glasses at the way people lived over there. Everything was bigger and bolder, a freedom brought about by a country that had not been bombed or left without food and resources. Anything American was desirable: music, films, fast-food and Coca-Cola – it all offered an escape. With this image of America in the heads of the planners and councils, the rebuilding of Britain was soon under way but, it was not just the bombed-out buildings that needed to be replaced. There was a whole new way of thinking which rippled through society and the media. From the Marlboro man to Elvis Presley, American heroes were looked up to by young Brits, and not many film-makers thought about the long-term effects of a people motivated by wealth and power. There was freedom embodied in the American way of life but, in Britain, freethinking 'Yanks' ruffled the feathers of the establishment in many fields, and this was true of Sydney before he even set foot in the country. Okay, so he was a Canadian, but what Englishman could tell the difference between a New Yorker and a Torontonian anyway?

One of the biggest talents that Grierson brought in was a fellow Scotsman called Norman McLaren whose anti-war film *Neighbours* won an Oscar in 1952. He was a pioneer in a number of areas including animation, visual music, abstract film, pixilation and graphical sound. Some of his earliest experiments with film saw him actually scratching and painting the film itself, and brought him to the attention of Grierson. McLaren is still remembered today as one of the great animators and, in recent years, a DVD box set of his work has been released, and an iTunes application – *McLaren's Workshop* – is also available. *Neighbours* gives a surreal representation of an argument between two men over a flower, and shows an escalating struggle for this thing of beauty until the men and the flower are killed.

In 1942, Sydney Newman suggested to Grierson that an animation department was needed to provide sequences for NFB documentaries. McLaren was asked to set one up. But there were no animators in Canada. McLaren went around the art schools. From both portfolios and interviews, he chose people he thought had animation potential. And McLaren chose wisely – Grant Munro, René Jodoin, George Dunning were amongst others. (McWilliams, 1990).

The films they made highlighted pretty much every aspect of war, but it was not all death and armies. Features such as *Neighbours* challenged the viewer to think outside the box, and like Sydney McLaren loved to approach a challenge from a different angle. By producing such poignant and thought-provoking situations, the idea was that the viewer would respond on an emotional level. There were so many big questions out there which the camera could show and, during his time at the NFB, Sydney was always looking for new ways to tell the big stories. There was a desire to show people things that evoked a guttural response, or tried to bring some sense to the unanswerable. In science fiction and surrealism, he found an answer and a way to tell a tale.

It was a seven-days-a-week job, and pulling such shifts was not uncommon for Sydney throughout his career. Later on, family life was much the same, holiday time being the exception to the rule.

All the time, there was pressure for his work to put out the right message and grab the audiences, and there was always the challenge of finding new ways to tell a story. They did features on everything; from recruitment videos to paper-drives, they put messages out across the country. On May 20, 1944, Sydney married Betty and things went along just fine for a while longer until the war ended and Grierson left. His wartime job as a minister of the Wartime Information Board, as well as being a consultant to the Prime Minister, was at an end. In 1945, he was dismissed from his post as Commissioner of the NFB when it was alleged that he was a Communist sympathiser. Russian Igor Gouzenko (who was living in Canada at the time) defected with secret papers showing Soviet spying activities and the names of spies in Canadian society, and it caused a panic. Grierson's name was discovered in Russian paperwork and his career never recovered. FBI files later revealed the harassment he had to endure as he became one of the first victims of the post-war scare tactics (Cox, 1979). After he was dismissed by the NFB, alongside three of his colleagues, it was Ross McLane who became the boss.

When the war ended, things began to change in the old country, with increasing investment from the USA in air and naval bases. Canada started to become prosperous again and, in 1948, the British Government gave the people of Newfoundland the choice, via a referendum, of remaining under British rule, becoming independent, or entering the Canadian confederation – which was what they chose to do. Sydney stayed on at the

Film Board after the war, but Grierson took some of the old team to New York with him. In peace-time, the board had to re-establish its role in the world, and the after-effects of war and new-found freedom were some of the subjects they explored. The rehabilitation of people, and the subject of post-traumatic stress disorder, was shown 35 years before the American Psychiatric Association added it to their diagnostic manual. Some of the survivors were mentally scarred, and such psychological problems were in their minds and bore an influence on the 1950s and 1960s, and, of course, had a bearing on the makers of films and television and radio shows. Peace was what people were looking for and, for a while, they thought they had found it, but war continued in places like Korea and Vietnam. People were still killing one another; it appeared nothing was really learned from the Second World War, and science fiction and drama were good mediums to highlight these problems. Setting them in a different context took out the sting. Many great engineers, scientists, and inventors were inspired by shows created by people like Sydney and others, such as Rod Serling, and Gene Roddenberry.

The premise of shows like *Doctor Who* and *Star Trek* is to tell stories about good reigning over evil, of discovery and freedom in space, but poignant and meaningful science fiction needs to have more than this to be considered great. Over the years,

Doctor Who has achieved its original aim of educating and showing something new when other shows have failed. Sydney wanted the Doctor to be out there amongst the stars, but to never lose his mystery. His Doctor was more than 700 years old so he had calmed down quite a bit, and this was before the concept of regeneration was invented. He was an elder statesman; Sydney never saw him as reactionary, a trait the character developed later on as younger actors took on the role. Overreaching everything, he wanted to see good stories, not just about flying saucers and planets; he wanted people to be challenged mentally and emotionally. The viewer should be able to relate to or be disgusted by ideas which, in ordinary everyday society, appear revolutionary, unnatural, or treasonous because of the law or prejudices and stereotypes of the times in which they were created.

In 1944, Sydney got the job as an executive producer of *Canada Carries On* and Betty was also working at the NFB. In her time with them, she was a writer, technical-coordinator, and chief negative cutter (Pratley, 1981) so, with two decent wages coming in, there was no longer a struggle. Sydney's feet were firmly under the table, which is exactly where he did not want them to be. He wanted to be battling the enemy, and outsmarting the big bosses to produce breathtaking, thought-provoking films. He was also sure that television was where the future was at, although he was grateful to be doing what he was doing. Another notable film he directed, in 1944, was a 12-minute feature called *The Trainbusters* which featured Canadian airplanes involved in an all-night bombing mission and destroying German munitions trains.

After the hostilities ended, he did not renew his interest in Disney; that was now a world away, although America would soon enough be calling him. Not as an artist, though – now he was directing, producing and making films that hundreds of thousands, even millions, of people saw so what more could he want?: to satisfy the ambition to make drama which challenged people's mind-sets and showed them the truth, and it all started here. In the end, he laid down foundation stones for some of the most versatile TV drama formats ever devised. There could be no bigger canvas on which to paint a story than the whole of time and space. It was not until 1966, when Patrick Troughton replaced Hartnell as the Doctor, that viewers saw how dynamic the show really was, although regeneration was not Sydney's idea. Not only could the scenery, settings, and accompanying characters be absolutely anything and anyone at all, the lead actor could change, too. It did not come much more ingenious than that. Other science-fiction shows have tried to copy the format, but to do it successfully, they always draw parallels to *Doctor Who*.

There were a lot beautiful ideas and places out there to make films about, but there was also a lot of doom and gloom, especially in Britain, after the war. It had settled there during the 1930s, and been intensified by the conflict. The escapism of the movies white-washed over some of the grittiness of reality. Everyday people faced desolation, bombed-out cities, and hearts aching for the ones they had lost. The world was changing fast and Sydney would pick up *The New Scientist*, or a similar journal, to keep up with what was going on. The hard job, of course, was catching the zeitgeist, writing something topical with far-reaching implications. Now that he was the one picking the directors and writers, he was pleased that he would now have a direct influence on how shows were made and what they put into it.

Many of Sydney's teachers had now gone and the films that Sydney and his colleagues made under Ross McLane were good, but they were not drama. The NFB would never match Hollywood blockbusters with stars such as Bette Davis, Kathryn Hepburn, and James Cagney, and Sydney was frustrated that his films were not getting out to a wide enough audience. It was then that he really began to think about moving across into television.

Hollywood had the film industry wrapped up but, by the 1940s, a fair number of Canadian people had TV sets in their living rooms, and they were able to tune into stations broadcasting from the USA. It was then that Sydney was asked to go on loan to NBC for 12 months and live in New York, and he jumped at the chance. It was a city that he felt he already knew so well because of the films he had seen and comic books he had read. The Big Apple was where all of the action took place, and now he would be there amongst it himself to pick up tips on how NBC made television. He was going on the front line, so to speak, and the offer was just too good to refuse.

Chapter Seven
New York and the Communists

After marriage, came children for Sydney and Betty, and three daughters – Deirdre, Jennifer, and Gillian – were born after the war. They would become used to moving around as their father took on jobs in different places, and would experience different cultures and ways of life. Ever supportive of her husband, Betty was the foundation stone that Sydney missed so much in his later years, after she died. It is also fair to say that he was not family orientated at this point in his life, but he loved his wife and children with all of his heart, and they did have memorable times with their father as they grew up. The problem was that he was forever working. To say he lived for work would not have been an understatement; he seemed to never be able to say 'no' to a new job. There were many occasions throughout his career when he had a considerable work-load and still took on more. This, of course, was at the expense of family life, but that is how it was for him. He missed so many gatherings and birthday parties as the children grew up because there was always a deadline looming.

Founded by David Sarnoff in 1926, National Broadcasting Company, or NBC, is the oldest broadcasting company in the USA, and Sydney was delighted to have the chance to take the family to New York for a year and work there. The company had started in television at the end of the 1930s, and their first network programme soon followed. By the time, he arrived, they had been making programs for a decade and had really refined the art. In those early days, everything was done live; producers and directors lived on their nerves and there was no scope for things to go wrong.

A first in science fiction history happened in America in the summer of 1949 when Sydney was there and, even though it was not made by NBC, it was one of a number of shows that Sydney had access to and would have had an influence on him when he produced a similar show called *Space Command* four years later.

Captain Video and His Video Rangers, *which premiered 27 June 1949 on the DuMont Network, was the first science fiction or space adventure programme on television and was to inspire a spate of similar offerings. Although it combined many of the early staples of children's programming, such as the inclusion of inexpensive film clips and pointed moral lessons,* Captain Video *capitalised upon the public fascination with science and* space and the technical elements of the new television medium to create the longest running science-fiction show in early television.

Captain Video *was the creation of James L. Caddigan, a DuMont Vice-President. Set in the year 2254, the show was an ambitious undertaking – it was live, technically demanding, and programmed as a continuing serial appearing every evening from 7 to 7.30pm. The show was designed to take advantage of the new technology; dissolves, superimpositions, and crude luminance key effects were utilised to place Captain Video in fanciful surroundings and allow him to travel through space and time. Without the luxury of videotape and editing, however, scripts, written by Maurice C. Brock (a veteran radio scriptwriter for* Dick Tracy *and* Gangbusters*) had to contain a great deal of exposition to allow time to set-up for short bursts of action...*

As the 'Master of Science,' Captain Video was a technological genius, who invented a variety of devices including the Opticon Scillometer, a long-range X-ray machine used to see through walls; the Discatron, a portable television screen which served as an intercom; and the Radio Scillograph, a palm-sized two-way radio. With public concerns about violence in television programming, Captain Video's weapons were never lethal but were designed to capture his opponents (a Cosmic Ray

Vibrator, a static beam of electricity able to paralyse its target; an Atomic Disintegrator Rifle; and the Electronic Strait Jacket, which placed captives in invisible restraints). In testimony before Senator Estes Kefauver's subcommittee probing the connection between television violence and juvenile delinquency, Al Hodge, who had previously starred in radio's Green Hornet *and became Captain Video in 1951, noted that he did not even use the word 'kill' on the show.* (Williams-Rautiolla, 2005).

Because of such limitations, making *Doctor Who* around this time and putting it out live would have been impossible because of how technically difficult it was. Controlling robots and making spaceships crash in small spaces (such as at Lime Grove Studio D, where the show was first recorded) was extremely difficult and took a lot of preparation. Special effects such as ray-gun blasts would have been impossible during a live performance, and it was not until the late 1950s that the BBC had the ability to record their own shows and re-take scenes thanks to the availability of two-inch videotape. Throughout the 1950s and early 1960s, advances in the space-race captured people's hearts and made the production of a new prime-time 'outer-space' BBC science-fiction TV show inevitable. There were memos flying around about such an endeavor whilst the idea of *Doctor Who* was still brewing in

Sydney's mind so, when he pitched it to his bosses, they were not unaware of the genre.

After a few months, Sydney had handled everything from *The Sid Caesar Show*, to live boxing at Madison Square Gardens, as well as drama at NBC (CBC Press Service, 1957). It was an exhausting learning-curve, but an amazing experience. He even worked on outside broadcasts, and was able to gain an in-depth knowledge of how things worked at NBC whose high standards a Canadian television company would have to adopt; his knowledge was invaluable when the CBC started up. As the 1950s began, new men were taking up positions in preparation of the big TV switch-on, with some from the NFB jumping across from making films. In the beginning, Canadians who bought TV sets were able to tune in to the US only if they were close enough to the border, so it was inevitable that Canadian TV would follow. Having such a highly-regarded fellow countryman with such a good knowledge of American programs was a good thing for Sydney.

In 1950, Senator Joseph McCarthy shot to prominence with his anti-Communist propaganda, and he became the visible face of the cold-war tensions that were building by spreading fear amongst the American people. McCarthy helped create an unhealthy atmosphere in the country by suggesting that the

USA had been inundated with Soviet spies. People started to watch for co-workers and neighbours, and reporting on them if they had suspicions they were Communist sympathisers. It was another witch-hunt and stirred up similar feelings of hatred organisations like the Ku Klux Klan were doing in the south. Of course, Grierson himself had been ruined a few years before by such tales.

McCarthy went as far as stating that Communists had infiltrated President Harry S. Truman's administration and, in June 1950, a booklet called *Red Channels* was published by *Counterattack* containing the names of people in the entertainment industry believed to be Communists. The list included well-known figures such as Orson Welles, Leonard Bernstein and Burgess Meredith, and Sydney could have become tied up in the mass-hysteria too (Hilmes, 2010). He had links with the Communist Party himself, through the poster and artwork he did, and they were all over the NFB looking for Communist sympathisers. Surely his name had to be on the list even though he was not a Communist and his association with them had ended a long time before the war? He had worked for them because of the money, and the poster work was something he was good at. He was not devoted to the cause, and he was not planning on overthrowing the US government anytime soon. In the back of his mind he would have been a little fearful of being arrested and locked away. People he knew were losing their livelihoods, just like his great friend Grierson, and he half expected there to be a knock on the door and he would be taken away. In the newspapers every day were the names of stars and celebrities who had been questioned or arrested, but it was not just that the USA which was affected by this mass-hysteria. In Canada, the allegations that Communist sympathisers had infiltrated the NFB were still circulating, and this made the government rethink how the agency should be run (Ohayon, 2014). They were not quite burning people at the stake like they did at the Salem witch trials of 1692-93, but there were frightening parallels, and very little evidence other than paranoia and fear of outsiders.

Anti-Communist feelings had been building since the Second World War ended and things certainly ramped up when the Soviets exploded an atomic bomb in August 1949. There was a genuine concern that another war was just around the corner, and this feeling was long lasting. After Nazism, there was now a new threat and, a few weeks after the bomb was dropped, the Communists took control of China. At the start of the Korean War, Sydney produced an episode of *Canada Carries On* called *Thunder In the East* which used archive footage as it looked at post-colonial Asia. Leaders such as Mahatma Gandhi were promoting democratic ideas and philosophies but the

Communist threat was always there, lurking in the shadows. It did seem like they were taking over the world for a while, with little or no regard for human rights, and the media helped drum up this fear. At any moment, America could be invaded. At least, that was the story the fear-mongers were trying to promote, and then the Soviet Union helped equip North Korea in the war against the South, who were backed by America. All of these things could now be viewed from the comfort of home on the family's TV set, but the Newman family did their best to just get on with things as they settled in New York. There was so much to see and do, and Betty would have kept the house and looked after the children all by herself as she didn't know anybody. Sydney would not have suddenly gone into vacation mode just because they were away from home – there was so much to see and do at NBC. The 1950s became a golden era of television, and for NBC, whose programme-making skills were amongst the best in the world.

From 1949 to 1950, Newman was assigned to NBC-TV in New York to research and compile a report to the Canadian government on American television techniques, especially in drama, documentary and outside broadcasting. In 1952, when the Canadian Broadcasting Corporation started its television service (CBC-TV), Newman was appointed supervising director of features, documentaries and outside broadcasts. (Vahimagi, 2014).

I worked with NBC for a year as an observer, and I sent back reports on the various phases of television. I spent four months in drama there, spent four months on remotes, and in the news department, and so on. It was a report I'd written on remotes which made the CBC offer me a job; they wanted me to do remotes for them. (Newman[3], 1966).

When they returned to Canada, Sydney had a head full of dreams and possibilities, but his burgeoning interest in television did not dull his passion for making films. His ambitions were sometimes above the budget and restriction of TV, and outside the remit of the NFB, so what could he do? Grierson had jokingly said to him, on numerous occasions, that he had the mentality of a B-movie director because he was always trying to keep things real and grounded for the viewer. He wanted them to react emotionally to what was happening, which implies Grierson did not think Sydney looked toward what would be considered spectacular, or the realm of blockbuster. The restrictions that he put on *Doctor Who*, like the non-inclusion of bug-eye-monsters, may well have been something that he would have dismissed even if the budget had been unlimited.

1951 was by far Sydney's most productive year up until that time. Excited by what was happening, and enjoying making films – he was producer, or executive producer of 14 that year, as well as directing *Talent Showcase*. One of the films he produced was *Screaming Jets* which was directed by Jack Olsen. It was 11 minutes long and designed to introduce Canada to the jet age, showing the world what airplanes they were developing. All the while, he was keeping tabs on the development of TV; he knew the Canadians were a million miles away from what he had seen in America, and they would really have to raise their game if they were going to get a station off the ground. Sydney had brought back information about the various techniques and methods used at NBC, including valuable information on outside-broadcasts. He had also developed a personal interest in dramas by this time, and he would soon get a chance to try his hand at producing one himself. On returning to the NFB from New York, he made *Eye-Witness No. 33*, and another 15 films would follow before he came to the end of his time at the organisation. Between 1943 and 1952, Sydney produced or directed at least 40 films for the board, but once he had his head turned by NBC, he knew that television was where he wanted to be. Film had been around for years, but TV was brand new in Canada and he had the chance to be involved right at the start.

Chapter Eight
Swapping Celluloid for Electrons

The 1950s was a golden era for science fiction, with ever more far-fetched ideas revealing themselves in each new film or series. Some of them were believable, others looked ridiculous, but now there were wrap-around big-screen cinemas, 3D, and animatronics to show the viewers the dangers of body-snatching, mind-melding, and alien invasion. Many have been remade in the late 20th, or in the 21st century using CGI, but some of the original films have stood the test of time, especially the ones that did not overreach themselves. Sydney was not convinced about monsters made from papier-mâché and rubber back then, and today they look awful. *Doctor Who* is littered with them. *The Web Planet* is a good example of such an over-ambitious story, although alien planets and their inhabitants have been portrayed effectively many times. The debut of the Cybermen in *The Tenth Planet* was excellent, despite their boots being sprayed silver, and the story is menacing and believable. Co-creator Doctor Kit Pedler was scientific advisor on *Doctor Who* when Innes Lloyd took over as producer in

1966. By then, the show was at a crossroads and the new production team had their own ideas about the direction it would go in now that Patrick Troughton was the Doctor, and they reported directly to Sydney, who had the final say.

Pedler was also the head of electron microscopy at the University of London, so he injected more hard science into the show. Discussions with script editor Gerry Davis on how science and technology could interfere and effect human life led to the creation of the Cybermen. It was a great time to be involved in television, and a good time to be working on *Doctor Who* if you had a creative mind. From transistors to DNA, the world was changing and Sydney did his best to keep up with scientific advancements, as well as current affairs. He had devoured newspapers, magazines, and books since he was a boy and, when he found time for the cinema, there was a plethora of movies to see from many genres. Each film was more daring than the last and, by the end of the 1950s, most of the major science-fiction themes had been covered. How such ideas could be transferred to television and made believable was the question he was about to ask himself.

Without Sydney's persistence and influence, Canadian and British television would have been worse off, although there were many times he felt out of his depth and he was down to earth enough to admit it. There were also the times when clashes in personalities and opinions occurred and, if an idea was stuck firmly in his head, you could be sure he had already have debated it and thought out all possible outcomes. He was not a jealous or controlling man and he knew a good idea when he saw it. Films such as *The Day the Earth Stood Still* (1951), which featured flying saucers and a robot called Gort, and *The War of the Worlds* (1953), with its amazing special-effects, were two of the biggest hits of the era. On seeing these, Sydney set out to discover how a production of such magnitude could be scaled down and made for television. Film-makers had the luxury of time and re-takes if something went wrong, and there was a budget of $2 million (around $19 million in 2017 money) for director Byron Haskin's spectacular adaption of H.G. Wells' book, *The War of the Worlds*, which became the biggest science-fiction hit of the year.

The small screen could not hope to compete with such blockbusters, and these movies showed a divide which has always existed between film and TV science fiction. Evidently, the release of *Star Wars* in 1977 was not the first time it had been observed, although George Lucas's film raised the benchmark significantly. Shows such as *UFO* and *Space 1999* were totally outclassed and *Doctor Who* was left looking like the poor relative. This difference is not so apparent today but, back then, a lot of TV stories focused on characters and their situations, more than effects. Good stories that taxed the mind, or turned normality on its head, usually made up for the poor special effects, but Sydney was of the opinion they should not make it if it was not believable. A far greater picture could be created by leaving the viewer imagining a monster or a killer, rather than showing them a man in latex with the spray-painted wellies. It had to be believable, and monsters and dinosaurs rarely looked real before advances in CGI and the release of *Jurassic Park* in 1993. The early days of the Canadian Broadcasting Corporation who Sydney joined when his contract at the NFB came to an end were a million miles away from this world.

One of Newman's reports on outside broadcasting was seen and admired by executives at the Canadian Broadcasting Corporation (CBC) and, in 1952, he joined the Corporation as their Supervising Director of Features, Documentaries and Outside Broadcasts. There, he was involved in producing, not only some of the earliest television editions of Hockey Night in Canada, *but also the first Canadian Football League game to be shown on television. After his experience of seeing the production of television plays in New York, he was eager to work in drama despite, by his own admission, "knowing nothing about drama." He was nonetheless able to persuade his superiors at CBC to make him Supervisor of Drama Production in 1954. In this position, he encouraged a new wave of young writers and directors, including Ted Kotcheff and Arthur Hailey, and oversaw shows such as the popular* General Motors Theatre. (Graham, 2016).

When the Canadian Broadcasting Corporation started their television service in 1952, it was a new beginning. Hollywood had the monopoly on films, but television was a different matter. Sydney had seen enough to know what an audience wanted to see; it was what he wanted, too; what made them scream and laugh and hide their eyes before gasping in amazement at the wonderment before them on the screen. He had always been intrigued by H.G. Wells' book *The Time Machine*, and watching Rod Taylor's excellent portrayal of the inventor in the 1960 movie was instrumental in him choosing the path that lead him towards *Doctor Who*. It is just that the moment was not as significant for him as it was for some; it steamrollered as the years went by into the modern show today. Having ideas was all well and good but tea-time science fiction was a complete unknown and, after the production crew had switched off the lights and gone home, there was still some worrying left for Sydney to do.

As supervising-producer of outside broadcasts, Sydney could be asked to make shows from any location in Canada, and this was quite a challenge. He had joined CBC-TV Toronto before it started broadcasting on September 8, 1952, two days after the Montreal service began. Much to the embarrassment of those involved, they displayed the opening image (the station's call letters, CBLT) upside down and the wrong way around but, other than this, Sydney found he was working with professional people, many of whom he knew, such as Ross McLane and Harry Rasky (Strange, 1977) so he was not, by any means, the only creative talent. Technical people had been over to Britain to visit the BBC and watch how they did things, and the sports events Sydney had covered helped him when he first started at the CBC and he was asked to produce shows such as *Hockey Night*. Still, there was concern over how they were going to run the service, and they were not able to attract the money and sponsorship that NBC had. They could always use the BBC as a benchmark, but some of their standards were something to work towards, rather than achieve overnight. This became a two-way relationship, and the BBC eventually started to buy Canadian programmes to show to the British public. When this happened, it would have been seen as a seal of approval by Sydney and his contemporaries. In Cy Strange's CBC Television Special from 1977, Director of BBC Television, George Barnes, addresses the Canadian people in 1952 in a well-received English accent, and he comments on how confident he is that Canadians will be able to make good television. Looking at it now, it appears rather condescending, although, at the time, this would have been seen as a pat on the back from the mother country to the fledgling CBC, who were still largely winging it.

Gather the family and warm up the television! On September 8, 1952, CBC Television makes its historic debut... Broadcasting from a studio in Toronto, a nervous and excited team of journalists and entertainers offers the first evening's entertainment. Canadians laugh at a three-puppet sketch featuring the eccentric character Uncle Chichimus. A young Glenn Gould dazzles the audience with a performance. And, CBC TV presents its first scoop with a news story about the Boyd Gang's break from the Don Jail. (CBC Digital Archive).

Lorne Green's reporting on the Boyd Gang on that first day was over-dramatic, like something out of a western, which suggested that the CBC were not quite too sure in which direction they were going at the start. If Lorne was going to be seen as a serious presenter or news anchor, like those on American television, he had to knock off the 'High Noon' routine. There were, naturally enough, teething problems when they started out but, on the whole, the newspapers gave a thumbs-up to the opening night, barring the mistake with the test card, and, by 1954, there were almost 700,000 television sets in Canada. After a while, things began to settle down and the station ran smoothly. They started to make some good programmes, such as *Let's See* and *The Wayne and Shuster Hour*, and Silvio Narizzano's version of *20,000 Leagues Under the Sea* which went out live for six weeks from September 13, 1952.

When it began in '52, they had gathered together this group of about 20 of us who had come from everywhere. From radio – well, I was from the film-board – and none of us knew a hell of a lot, although I had spent a year with NBC in New York. It was terribly exciting, and nobody had any yardstick by which to judge, therefore almost anything could go... We fed off one another's enthusiasm, and everything built up, and we pioneered in every which way...

We had a group of about nine directors. I was the producer of all the shows, as well as the supervisor of drama, and we had a good thing. I had a marvelous team... We all were excited and dedicated about getting original writing. (Newman[3], 1966).

Sydney wore many hats during his time at the CBC, and it is true to say that he had an influence on things that may have been outside his remit, as well as putting together his shows. In the past, he had been a bit of a jack-of-all-trades, which helped him because he knew how to talk to artists, stage designers, and lighting technicians. He had to co-ordinate the different roles of so many different people under his wing and he had to keep a cool head. He also had to try and be receptive and creative, and one of the things he told directors was that the close-up of the human face was the most natural subject for a TV picture (CBC Press Service, 1957). Sydney also worked with Samuel Nathan Cohen at the station; and Cohen became a story editor and another big influence on his career. Without his input, Sydney believed he may never have left Canada and gone to England to work. In his usual modest way, he said that his reputation was largely due to Cohen, who had also introduced him to the writer Arthur Hailey. Sydney gave Hailey his big break when the CBC bought his script *Flight into Danger* (Toronto Telegraph, 1971) and he went on to big things.

Part of the outside broadcast remit was a series of ten science shows which took place at the University of Toronto, where a stage-hand called Ted Kotcheff had just graduated in literature. He had been badgering Sydney for a while, and when he asked him if he could write the series, he was shocked when told he could. It was another calculated risk but, if Sydney perceived somebody to be clever and keen, he would do what he could. Even though he had to do quite a bit of re-writing, he could see that Kotcheff had talent and the youngster learned so much from him. The best piece of advice that Sydney gave him was about documentary-making, and he told him that the narrator should always say something different to what was in the pictures because this would give the audience two pieces of information at the same time and hold their interest; Ted figured out that this method also worked in drama. When CBC first went live, they had no head of drama, so they asked Sydney to take on the role and, although he admired such works, at the time he knew very little about making them. As a graduate of literature, he asked Ted to become his story editor, and, after about a year, he told Ted that he was a good writer, and that he had all of the skills to direct. This how Ted's career began, and he went on to direct many Hollywood films including *First Blood*, *Uncommon Valor* and *Weekend at Bernie's*.

They achieved many firsts in the fledgling years of the CBC and there was also an interest in science fiction. Canada went on to produce some of the best-known science fiction shows of all time. In recent years, there has been *The X-Files*, *Battlestar Galactica* and the *Stargate* franchise, and, of course, there is Sydney and *Doctor Who*. The only episode of the original show to be shot in Canada was the 1996 TV movie, which was filmed in Vancouver and starred Paul McGann. Canada was, however, the first North American country to air *Doctor Who* when the series began in 1964. It was a flop first time round and was cancelled after the conclusion of *Marco Polo*. The first Canadian 'space' show aired only six months after CBC-TV opened – *Space Command*, which was set on a space-station operated by Worldwide Command. The special-effects were arranged by John D. Lowry, who went on to work on *Star Wars*, and he set up the department at the CBC. Cutting his teeth on such shows, he produced rocket launches and weightless astronauts, and went on to develop The Lowry Process of film restoration in 1977 which has been used on many famous movies. In all 150 episodes of *Space Command* went out between 1953 and 1954 and featured future *Star Trek* actors James Doohan and William Shatner. The show was remarkable because each of the 30-minute episodes were live.

Several Canadian shows were purchased by the BBC, including the episode of the *General Motors Theatre* called *Flight to Danger* in 1956, which featured James Doohan as an ex-Spitfire ace who takes control of a jumbo jet after the pilots fall ill and it is about to fly through a storm. It was these shows that first got Sydney known in Britain.

Up to 1958, I was head of drama for the Canadian broadcasting corporation, and the BBC, for reasons of its own, bought 26 of my Canadian plays which were one hour in length and ran them on the BBC. There was my name at the end of every one, 'supervising producer Sydney Newman', and so my name got known here a bit. And then crosscut to ABC television. Howard Thomas wanted to promote Dennis Vance and asked him if he could find a replacement for himself. That's how I was found and interviewed, and flown to England and wined and dined and I accepted the job as head of drama for ABC Television. (Newman[2], 2006)

That fact is I was not tired of Canada, or anything like that. I think I became tired of being a producer in television (at CBC). I'm using the word producer, not as a director… A director stages the actors before the camera… The term 'producer' in my sense, in Canada, would be a supervising producer. I really think I was fed up with being a supervising producer of programs. Also, I was faced with two choices: one was to eventually get out of television, but when the opportunity came to work in television in another country, I thought this might this might be okay. The fact is, I'm obviously a very unstable guy, anyone who starts out as a painter, and then becomes a film-maker, and then gets into documentary-type-television, and then ends up being a drama-chief, there must be something very restless about me. In fact, I really want to play the flute someday. (Newman[3], 1966).

Chapter Nine
Time and Space

A pioneering US children's puppet series called *Howdy Doody* started on NBC just after Christmas 1947, and CBC went on to make their own version. It set a precedent for ventriloquist TV productions after originally starting out on radio as a sketch. It was dreamt up and voiced by 'Buffalo' Bob Smith, and Howdy Doody himself was a cowboy puppet, similar to Woody from the *Toy Story* films. CBC's version of the show started in November 1954 and it ran for five years, with James Doohan and William Shatner again involved as Rangers Bill and Bob. Sydney oversaw its production, and he later recalled a puppet character called Mr X who was described in the CBC Television production notes for the show below from November 1954:

Howdy Doody, the happy, boyish puppet, comes to the CBC-TV network November 15, with his friends in the imaginary town of Doodyville...

Chief trouble-maker in Doodyville is a puppet character, Phileas T. Bluster. He's more a killjoy, than a villain, keeping the townsfolk in a state of annoyance over his crotchety behaviour. A fabulous puppet character called Mr X contributes mystery and excitement to the Canadian show, whizzing backwards and forwards in time and space in his 'Whatsis Box and peeking at history along the way.

This idea was not a million miles away from *Doctor Who*, even though the character Mr X appeared only in the early shows, and was removed because parents rang the station to complain that he was scaring the children. In the end, the show was cancelled for the same reason, but Mr X has a lot of similarities to the Doctor. A sense of mystery, and the idea of travelling incognito, has been the way of pirates, adventurers and cowboys for as long as man could think and connive, usually hiding their identities to escape justice. *Doctor Who* has always tried to protect the lead character's anonymity; he is always the mysterious outsider, just like those buccaneers and gunslingers, or those poor refugees back on Queen Street. The fact that this puppet travelled through time and space in a 'Whatsis' Box, and taught children about history, is too similar to the original to *Doctor Who* not to have had an influence on Sydney, but that did not mean to say he was trying to sell the idea from then on in.

By 1954, Sydney had a huge work-load, and there would have been very little time for anything else. Always looking outwards at the world as it forever changed, his own little brood was developing, too, and it was not easy having a father who was usually preoccupied as they grew from children into teens. The responsibility of *Ford Television Theatre* and *General Motors Theatre* was a huge one, although many fine directors were brought on by Sydney and the team during this time, including Ted Kotcheff, Alvin Rakoff and Silvio Narizzano. Always, tough, was the task of juggling the needs of the artist with the demands of the sponsors. When this was achieved, he would have to sit down and see if it could be done, or they would be violating broadcasting laws; he could not just do what he wanted. His biggest talent was keeping everybody calm and not appearing wound-up himself. Sydney's was a quiet and confident authority, with a tongue like a razor when it needed to be used. Usually he would sit there and listen, a leg crossed or a foot resting on the top of a desk, as he puffed on a cigarette.

I got along so well with the General Motors people. We had terrible rows, but basically, I found a good sense generally prevailed... I never felt profound discontent along those lines. When I worked at the film-board, we had restrictions but I worked within them and it never barred me from being creative (Newman[3], 1966).

For the series *On Camera*, they managed to get the actor Donald Pleasance and English script-writer John Lucarotti, whose career was just beginning. He also went on to write six stories for Sydney's The Avengers series between 1961 and 1965, as well as penning the *Doctor Who* serials *Marco Polo*, *The Aztecs*, and *The Massacre of St Bartholomew's Eve*. In total, he wrote 15 episodes, working under producers Verity Lambert and John Wiles between 1964 and 1966, and was also responsible for the original script for The Ark in Space in 1974 which was extensively re-written by Robert Holmes. He also wrote all three of the Target novelisations for his televised stories. He passed away in 1994 at the age of 68 from spinal cancer

In 1955, age just 23, Ted Kotcheff became CBC'S youngest director, and he had a sharp mind and was a quick learner. He stayed at the station until 1958, when he moved to England and ended up working with Sydney again on *Armchair Theatre* until 1960. He made his first film, *Tiara Tahiti*, a comedy with James Mason and John Mills, two years after that. He was never asked by Sydney, or anybody else, to work on *Doctor Who*; it would not have been a natural progression for him. In retrospect, it seems like a missed opportunity for the team. Ted showed, early on, that he was a talented, but *Armchair Theatre* was the last show he did with Sydney. At the time, he would have viewed 'children's' TV as a step backwards, but he may have done it for Sydney if he had picked up the phone.

Looking at *Doctor Who* now as a global brand is very different to how Ted saw it at the time, and he has never been familiar with the show, other than knowing it was Sydney's creation. His career took him to Hollywood, where *Doctor Who* was unknown until Tom Baker's episodes showed on PBS in 1978, and it gained cult-status. By 1967, Ted was making TV movies like *The Human Voice*, with Ingrid Bergman, and *The Desperate Hours*, with George Segal. He went on to direct many films, and *First Blood* (1982) with Sylvester Stallone as Vietnam veteran John Rambo made more than $47million. Perhaps the biggest drama of his directing career happened during an ill-fated live episode of *Armchair Theatre* in 1958.

The production in question was Underground, *transmitted on Sunday, November 30, 1958 as part of ITV company ABC's popular* Armchair Theatre *drama anthology. It was directed by William (known as 'Ted') Kotcheff, one of ABC's regular directors, then aged only 27, and produced by Sydney Newman, who had recently been given responsibility for all the company's drama. The play was a television dramatisation by James Forsyth of Harold Rein's novel* Few Were Left, *which had been published in 1955. No recording of the play exists, so this account is based on various interviews and media reports about the play. There are several accounts of what happened which, though largely consistent on the main events, differ notably on the smaller details...*

The ill-fated actor was Welshman Gareth Jones. Accounts differ as to his age, with The Times, The Manchester Guardian, The Daily Mirror, The Daily Express *and* The Stage *newspaper all reporting he was 35, whereas fellow actors Peter Bowles (who appeared in* Underground*) and Richard Huggett (who, to the best of our information, did not) put him in his twenties. Kotcheff reported he was 32. In their obituary,* The Stage *called Jones "A good actor, a hard worker, a real 'pro and a man of great personal charm." Decades later, Huggett, who reported he had been Jones's friend and contemporary at drama school, recalled him as "a fat, flabby, lazy, likable, oversexed, boozy, moderately talented actor."*

The Manchester Guardian *reported that, after Jones complained of feeling unwell, "he lay down to rest and died shortly after." All sources agree that Jones died of a heart attack. Kotcheff reported being advised initially only that Jones had passed out, and then, shortly afterwards, being told that he had died.* The Daily Mirror *noted that Jones was attended by a doctor visiting the studio, but to no avail. This latter detail is explained by Peter Bowles's later recollection that a doctor and nurse were on hand in case of accidents caused by the large amount of rubble strewn across the studio as part of the set. The extent of the interval between Jones's collapse and his death is unclear but indications are that it must have been brief.* (Wake, 2013)

By the end 1950s, Sydney was by no means the finished article, and was still willing to listen and learn, although he was very familiar with Canadian television, of course, maybe even too familiar. Getting it right was the difference between success and failure, and shows were still going out live. There was no option of a re-take so, as much as possible had to be worked out in the rehearsals. He was not necessarily looking for a move at that point in his career, although he would have been foolish not to have listened to any offers. All the while, his schedule was gruelling; nobody could run at that pace for too long without a break, and Betty would have known this. There were still plenty of good times ahead; it was not work all of the time. Scores of executive dinners, dances and award ceremonies were to come, but most of the time, they were both working. Betty in the home, and Sydney could be anywhere; his was a career which never stood still.

It was whilst he was on a trip to England that Sydney was offered the job at ABC, and he could not help but be excited by the chance to work in British television, and they seemed like the kind of bosses who would not restrict his creativity. The worked had got him noticed by people in the right places, and this is when he first got an offer to come and work in England.

"The productions impressed Howard Thomas, who was the managing director of ABC, the franchise holder for the rival ITV network in the English midlands and the north at weekends. Thomas offered Newman a job with ABC as a producer of his own Saturday night thriller series, which Newman accepted, moving to Britain in 1958. In 1975, the Head of Drama at the CBC, John Hirsch, noted that the tendency of so many writers and directors having followed Newman to the UK in the 1950s and never having returned to work in Canada had a detrimental impact on the standard of subsequent Canadian television drama." (Graham, 2016)

When Sydney came to England, and when he started to assemble the production crew for *Doctor Who*, he was looking for talent, and it did not necessarily need to come from the establishment. He was aware of the class-structure in Britain, but he did not give a damn – as long as they could do the job, that was all that mattered. He was not interested in their gender or ethnicity, and he didn't give a hoot about what anyone else thought. This was a forward way of thinking at a time when women, Asians and blacks were considered second-class citizens. Sydney had been an outsider all of his life and, from this perspective, came some of his best ideas. The original wanderer. But what about the wanderer in the fourth dimension? The idea for *Doctor Who* did not come about overnight, and was not his first attempt at science fiction. One thing is for sure, Sydney would have happily stood at the controls of the TARDIS and flown it off into the unknown, but whether that would be into the past, or into the future, will never be known.

The idea was that Sydney and the family would come over to England for two years and, now in his early 40s, he felt like this was too good an opportunity to pass up. It would certainly offer him more opportunities, but he knew that the job would not be easy. London was a city like no other; the fashion and the music, the sheer pace of the place, was so different to Toronto. People talk about the demise of the British Empire, and if this is so, then the late 1950s and 1960s was its reprieve. Everything was changing and Britain was lifting itself out of a post-war slump as gleaming housing estates and shopping centres started shooting up all over the land. Towering slabs of concrete, some at obscure angles – what were the architects putting in their pipes these days? Out of the decimation of the Blitz, a new Britain was born, and for a while, everyone thought they really could change the world for the better. Sydney's world was full of newness and hope, endless possibilities arising from broken dreams and promises. If only he could have seen into his own future. In a few short years, he would revolutionise British television, and nobody could have predicted any of it.

I left [CBC] for purely personal and selfish reasons, and I don't say that in any self-critical way, either. Each of us has to find, and bring out the best in ourselves, to extend oneself. I had given the drama there a good run; I was offered a job in a country I'd heard a great deal about, England; as we all had as children, and it was a chance to give my three children a taste of another country, different tradition, different cultural climate. It was an interesting job they had offered me; in fact it was exactly the same as the job I had in Toronto. (Newman[3], 1966)

Dennis Vance had become the first head of the ABC when the company started transmitting in 1955, and ITV began their planning for the new channel after the Television Act was passed the year before and this broke the BBC's monopoly. A consortium of television companies was founded to control programmes in various regions, but one of them (Kemsley-Winnick TV) collapsed soon after the franchise was granted and ABC was created to take its place. They were responsible for programme-making in the Midlands, and in the North of England, and the first broadcast was a live ceremony from the Guildhall in London on September 22, 1955. Back then, shows were not sponsored like some are today; there were only the commercial breaks. Controllers and programme-makers were not as aware of the balance between what was being sold and the content of the show, although it would not have made sense to screen an advert for a new car before a programme containing a car-crash. ITV's approach was less sensitive than America's, and Sydney was aware of this. The restrictions which had pinched him when he made shows such as the *General Motors Theatre* were not so apparent, although he did know how to broker compromises between the sponsor and the director. ABC operated out of three sites around the UK for more than 12 years, before merging with Rediffusion in 1967 to form Thames Television.

Fortunately, Dennis Vance had left *Armchair Theatre* in a good position, and Sydney would be producing this, as well as heading up the drama department. Born in Birkenhead in 1924, Vance had at first been an actor, and in the 1948 film *Scott of the Antarctic* which starred John Mills, played Charles S.

Wright, a Canadian member of the expedition. It is interesting to note that future *Doctor Who* producer Barry Letts was also in the film; both men later gave up the limelight to work in production at the BBC in the 1950s. At ABC, Vance produced the live drama *Armchair Theatre* which was popular before Sydney took control of the show. None of Vance's episodes still exist as they went out live, and there was no way to record them, and he has been criticised in the past because he was more inclined to put-out adaptations of books and plays, rather than new material. Works by Edgar Allan Poe, and J. B. Priestley, are two examples, but the quality of the shows was very good and often gained rave reviews. *Armchair Theatre* filled the Sunday evening slot on ITV and was originally launched by Howard Thomas as serious drama. In 1959, production moved from Manchester to Teddington studios in London, where they were able to take advantage of videotape and record shows. Although video had been around since the beginning of the 1950s, it was not feasible to use until later in the decade, and, in the early 1960s it revolutionised television. Advances meant that producers and directors could edit and splice, and it also gave them the chance to reshoot scenes where a serious mishap or mistake was made, although this was not cost-efficient. With these tools, some amazing action shows were made, and Sydney was delighted to have been there right at the start; the new technology gave him a lot more space in which he could create. In England, there would be a whole new set of challenges, and Sydney was ready for whatever was coming.

There were really two challenges, personal and professional, because I've always believed that any art I was interested in had to have a connection with the people, with the audiences. Obviously, I was at a terrific disadvantage. I didn't know much about England, except what I'd learnt at school, or seen in the movies. I made as many trips inside the country as I could, and I went up to Scotland and spent weeks up there. I went to Wales, and Cornwall, and Ireland, and so on, to get the feel of the place. Professionally, I didn't really like what I saw here on television, and it seemed to me that the problems were very simple. Most television drama in 1958, and when I say 'most', I mean 98 percent of it, consisted of either dramatisations of short-stories and novels, or consisted of hand-me-down theatre plays which were adapted for television. (Newman[3], 1966)

© Jeph Preece 2017

Specially commissioned for the occasion.

Life at the Film Board ©NFB

© NFB

Charlie Chaplin was one of Sydney's heroes; some of the earliest films he saw were made by him.

©NFB

Back to his roots – Sydney started out as a splicer-boy at the board

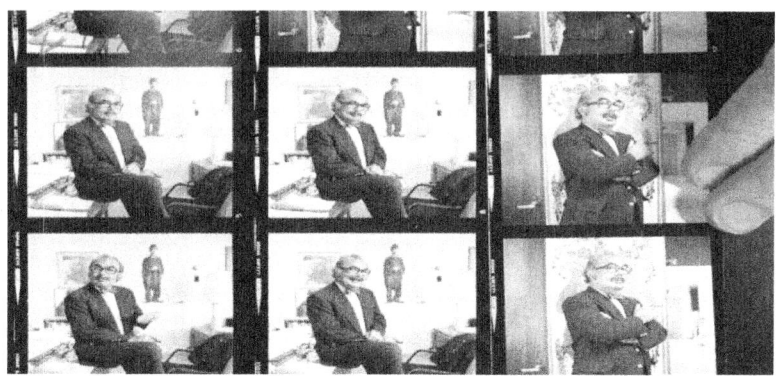

©NFB

©NFB - Seen here with John Grierson

©NFB - The desk job

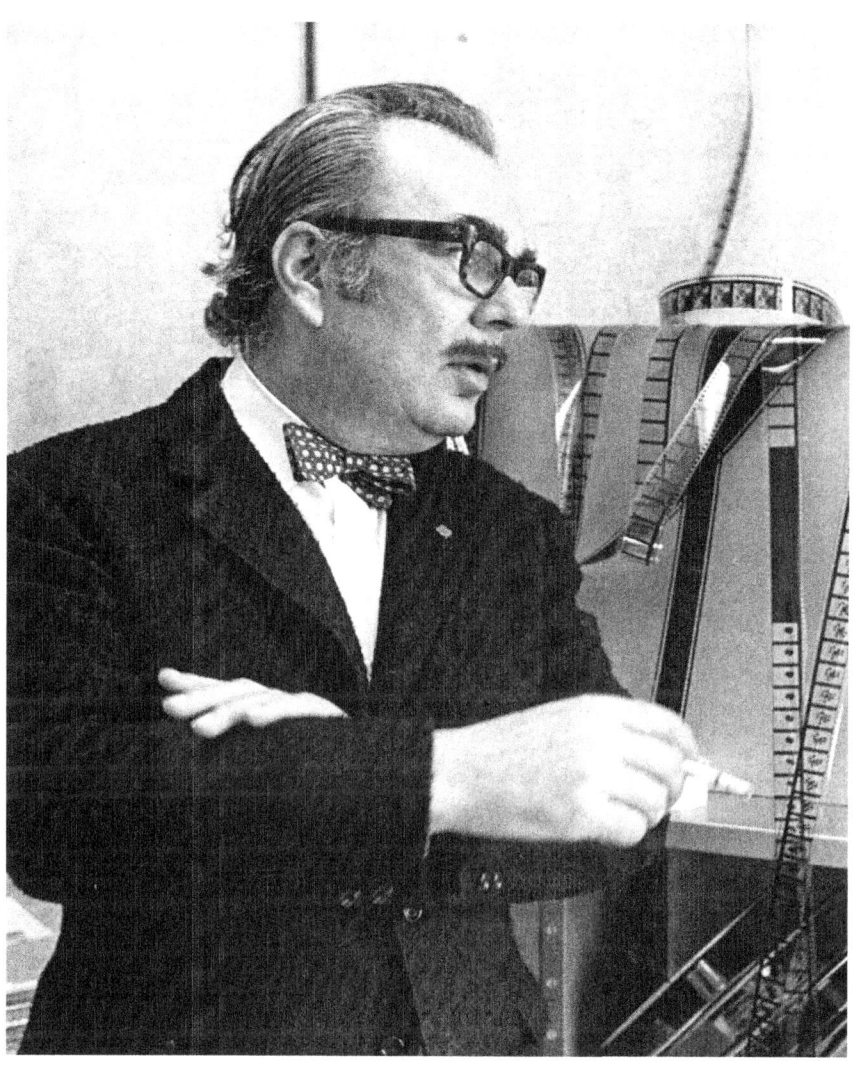

©NFB

The Man Who…

©NFB

...Thought Outside the Box

Chapter Ten
TV Revolution

Not only was the television revolution underway, new to the world was American rock 'n' roll, and a young generation of what the Press called 'teenagers' with bold new ideas and opinions. Rationing had ended in bleak old Britain several years before, and now the Brits were getting in on the 'showbiz' act. Musicians and film stars such as Cliff Richard, Diana Dors, and Tommy Steele were popular, and shows such as *Come Dancing*, *The Good Old Days*, *Sunday Night at the London Palladium*, *Dixon of Dock Green*, *Crackerjack*, and *Hancock's Half Hour* were hits on both the BBC and ITV networks, although the ratings war was not yet underway. As the 1950s drew to a close, many new opinions and attitudes were breaking through into popular culture, and television was about to give a voice to those on the fringes of society who'd never been heard before. US films were still dominant in the cinemas, but in 1958, there were British hits such as *Dunkirk*, *Dracula*, and *Carry on Sergeant* with William Hartnell. The fact that Hartnell felt type-cast in the sergeant-major role he played in the film, and in the TV series *The Army Game* (1957-61), was one of the reasons why he eventually accepted the role in *Doctor Who*. He was not producer Verity Lambert's first choice, and the character of the Doctor has evolved since it was conceived by Sydney, and portrayed by William. What the two men would have made of the show today is anyone's guess, but they would have surely marveled at the fact that it still be around in 2017, and through it their names have been kept alive.

Today's Doctor is a Time Lord, and a man of science and technology. His tinkering with Space and Time has made him a legend throughout the Cosmos, a far-cry from the cranky old man who hides his true identity. For Hartnell, it was the role he had been born to play until the relentless schedule took its toll. His was a new type of character, but the Doctors of today no longer seem lost like the old man who first appeared out of the mist. Neither is he truly wandering anymore, and he has complete mastery of the TARDIS which means it can usually land on a sixpence. These are just some of the factors that have eroded the mystery surrounding the Doctor, although, at its best, the show is a worthy successor, and it had to change to be accepted by today's audiences. Sydney realised the power of the Doctor's true identity right at the start, and that it should always be protected. Today's show gives the viewer the feeling that the Doctor's name is just beneath the surface, not hidden away in a Police-Box-time-machine sitting in a dark corner of a Totters Lane junkyard in London, 1963.

In those early stories, Hartnell's Doctor showed some mastery of machines and technology as a tool to aid the plot. Today, the devices and gizmos used in the show act as extensions of the character, just like our cellphones and tablets. Gadgets for spotting shape-shifting Zygons, and the ubiquitous Sonic-Screwdriver, provide a solution without an explanation, and leave the viewer in the dark. This makes for bad *Doctor Who*, and such methodology contributed to the death of the original series in 1989. Stories such as *The Happiness Patrol*, *The Greatest Show in the Galaxy*, and *Twin Dilemma* lacked depth of explanation, or over-complicated the plot, and seemed to ridicule the show's original premise, and its traditions at times. The later seasons sometimes made assumptions that the viewer already held certain information, e.g. that the Doctor was Merlin in *Battlefield*, or the complex relationship between Control, Light and Josiah Samuel Smith in *Ghostlight*. After his association with the BBC ended, Sydney would watch the show when it was on, but he didn't always like what he saw, and he died eight years before it was relaunched in 2005. Some of the later stories in particular appear farcical, and for him *Doctor Who* should never lose sight of its original premise. Always it should nurture the human spirit in its struggle for survival, no matter where it is in the Universe. Characters and personalities should shine through with aliens and machinery trailing someway behind.

After a few months at ABC Sydney could see that the company needed to change, and he started to set out his plans to his staff. People who were set in their ways and resisted such changes were shown the door, as were those who didn't want to make the shows he wanted to make. To start out with, he had an idea of what he wanted to do, and that became more definite as time went on. There were a lot of things he'd dealt with before at CBC and he could deal with most situations quite effectively, although he would have been operating in an alien environment but there was help for him and his family. There were quite a number of cultural differences that Sydney and Bessie would need to master if they were going to hob-nob with the executives and aristocrats. Never-the-less, Sydney was filled with optimism, and before long they had settled, with the children at school, and he really started to put into development some of his ideas. He hoped perhaps that his shows might have a positive influence on Great Britain, and give people a chance to alter some of their long-held mindsets, opinions, and beliefs. It was then that he began to realise just how huge his responsibility was.

Away from the studios he rarely mixes with TV people. His circle of close friends include several Canadians, where he entertains in a Victorian house in Hampstead brought up to date with central heating, and other Canadian style comforts. With his wife, who is the daughter of a Presbyterian missionary, and three daughters, he shares a cosy family life that keeps him clear of the London social whirl. He takes a lot of work home. (Greatorex, 1961)

Cliff Richard's *Move It* is credited with being one of the first authentic rock 'n' roll songs to be recorded outside of the USA, and it summed up well what was happening to Sydney and his family in 1958. There would be a great deal of changes to make, that was for sure, and things were less than certain in Great Britain. This was the year of the Munich Air disaster, where seven Manchester United players were amongst the twenty-one dead. There were protests for nuclear disarmament on Hyde Park Corner, and at Aldermaston in Berkshire, but by far the biggest problem was immigration. Towards the end of the 1940s it had been recognised that the reconstruction of Britain would require an influx of immigrant labour which arrived from the West Indies and Africa, causing prejudice and racial violence in Britain. After being in the job for a little while, Howard Thomas promoted Dennis Vance to the Head of Programme development, and he asked Sydney if he would like to take the post as Head of Drama. After the agreement had been made for him to also produce *Armchair Theatre* alongside his role, he signed the contract.

The series had been launched in 1956 and had proved very successful, but now ABC wanted Newman to bring to it the same qualities that he'd introduced in Canada. Newman accepted, not for financial reasons but because he felt it presented him with a new and irresistible challenge. He'd identified the same class differences that he'd come across in North America. 'At the time, I found this country to be somewhat class-ridden.' He later recalled. 'The only legitimate theatre was of the 'anyone for tennis' variety, which, on the whole, presented a condescending view of working-class people. Television dramas were usually adaptations of stage plays, and invariably about upper classes. I said 'Damn the upper-classes – they don't even own televisions!' My approach was to cater for the people who were buying low cost things like soap every day. The ordinary blokes the advertisers were aiming at.' (Laurence & Hulse)

Dennis Vance ended up stabbing a lover, in 1961, who rejected him and he received psychiatric help, but Sydney still thought highly of him. The occurrence happened during a break in camera rehearsals for *The Avengers* episode *Please Don't Feed the Animals*, which Vance was directing. Actors Ian Hendry and Patrick Macnee were having a lunchtime pint in a pub near Teddington Studios when Vance burst in, wielding a carving knife, and demanded to know the whereabouts of his girlfriend Janice Willett. He eventually found her in her office just as the tea-lady came around the corner pushing her trolley, and Vance knocked her to the side before nicking poor Janice in the cheek with the knife. After the assault, he was taken away for psychiatric help, but he eventually returned to work some weeks later, and subsequently had a long career both directing and producing for British TV, dying in 1983. There was also a new name doing the rounds by the name of Leslie Duncan. Her first UK writing credit was the *Armchair Theatre* episode called the *Witching Hour*, but she'd been with Sydney in Canada and written an episode of *The United States Steel Hour*. She was better known to Sydney as Betty Newman, his wife.

The drama department offices were situated in Film House on Wardour Street, Soho where the pubs and clubs were packed every night with writers and poets, actors, directors, and artists. This was a golden era for the creative industry in London with so many breakthroughs and firsts happening around this time. The Marquee Club was on the same street, having moved from its original location in Oxford Street where it first opened in 1958, and where the Rolling Stones gave their first performance in July 1962. Soho has, for a long-time, been seen as a trendy part of London, as well as the heart of the city's sex industry, and would have been somewhat reminiscent of Queen Street until the 1959 Street Offences Act came into force. Sydney had an idea of what he wanted to do with *Armchair Theatre*, but again not the complete picture. During his time in London he went to the pubs, clubs, and theatres, and listened to the people around him as he searched for new talent. He was sure it was out there, it would just take some time to establish contacts and channels of communication with managers, agents, and artists. He'd done all of this before back home in Canada with CBC, but this time things were different – he was a foreigner and an outsider in England. Fortunately his manners, and the 'American' accent did the trick, or at least stopped the door from being slammed in his face too often, although it was impossible to attract the top playwrights because the money in TV work wasn't good enough, so he had to go out and find his own.

It was then that a life-long friendship started between Sydney and Peter Luke, who was a genuine war hero, having won the Military Cross during the Second World War. After the conflict was over, he became a sub-editor on the Reuters news-desk before he slipped out of the business for ten years. He became a key member of the *Armchair* team, and Sydney could see that he had a unique eye for talent. Sydney made many changes designed to modernise the drama department and bring in new blood, and Peter was vital. Another Torontonian Alvin Rakoff, was also directing *Armchair* his first play *Man in the Corner* had aired earlier in the year, starring Jacqueline Hill who he had recently married. Like Ted Kotcheff, Alvin never directed any *Doctor Who*, despite his friendship with Sydney, and the fact that Jacqueline became a regular member of the original TARDIS crew as Barbara Wright, and she was married to Rakoff until her death in 1993.

What was it the shows were missing? Sydney couldn't quite put his finger on it as first – there was some good stuff, but it wasn't his sort of thing. His first play was *The Widower* by Cyril Campion, and he brought in Ted Kotcheff to do the next, *The House of Bernarda*. After a while he began to get a clearer picture of what he needed to do to make the show believable. At that time, there wasn't a great deal of difference between TV plays and theatre plays, and this was all wrong. At the theatre people could accept the limitations, such as a lack of effects and the limitations of the sets, but why was this so with TV plays? Sydney had seen how they were designed during his time in Hollywood, and he also knew they didn't have to cost the Earth, they just needed a bit of imagination. He needed to surround himself with his kind of creative types, and at the beginning of his time at ABC, and later at the BBC, he felt restricted at first. There were big changes to make at ABC, and BBC drama needed a major overhaul. Sydney needed to develop an angle to revitalise *Armchair Theatre* and take it in a new direction, and it was then that he started to think about what he could create, and introduce a sense of mystery and intimacy with close-ups. The cameras could get into places you couldn't hope to see in the theatre, and a good example of this is in the very first episode of *Doctor Who – An Unearthly Child* – when the Doctor encounters Ian and Barbara in the junkyard for the first time. It almost feels as if Hartnell is talking to the audience when he asks the schoolteachers who they are, and what they're doing, and the way the scene is shot makes the viewer feel as if they are intruding. Verity Lambert would have been keen to get it right after the pilot episode was rejected by Sydney, who ordered it to be re-shot.

You always have trouble getting material which you think is really fine enough. But the fact is, I remember when television started and they said "my God where will we get the actors from, where will we get the writers" and all this nonsense, the fact is they exist. What does exist is the opportunity, and television does provide the opportunity. In this country writers and actors, they just crawled out from under the rocks. (Newman[3], 1966)

Things began to change for Sydney at ABC after a while, and he was delighted to be getting new and original scripts. In the beginning, they dripped through, but he put out a call to every agent and writing group, and asked for recommendations. They were going to tell stories about the kinds of people that were actually sitting down to watch these shows, and he knew they would either love it or hate it. He wasn't going to ridicule them, or show how it could be if they had money – he was going to just show the world how they lived. What he was going to do was revolutionary in Britain, and there were people out there writing the types of story he wanted, and he had the power to sanction such shows allowing them to be seen by a large portion of the population.

I'd come here two years or so after John Osborne had written Look Back in Anger *which in my books was a terrific play and expressed the discontent of a burgeoning working class feeling its social, and intellectual oats. I determined I was going to get plays specially written for television, so that was essentially a craft-creative problem because dialogue for the theatre is usually too loud, and its written to be belted out. The acting is usually insincere, not to the audience in the theatre but, put that kind of acting in front of a camera and immediately it's too big.*

I set about to make sure that all the plays I used had: A, their origins in television, that is they would have a desire to express what they had to say within terms that were best for television. Secondly, because I always believed in a writer being quite close to the production, it automatically meant that my writers were English. (Newman[3], 1966)

What Sydney was looking for was original work, and new opening titles were also commissioned. He was confident in his plan because he knew what he was saying made sense, and that the targets he'd set everybody were achievable. He wasn't asking for the Earth, but it was going to be tough. Just like the formulation of *Doctor Who*, the advancement of *Armchair Theatre* and 'kitchen sink' drama was a mixture of Sydney's original vision, and the work of others. Another contributing factor was the fact that he was in the right place at the right time, with a wealth of experience at his disposal. It took him a little while but he found a balance, and was able to keep Howard Thomas and other senior members of ABC staff at arms-length and off the backs of the creative people. He knew they would work best as long as they weren't being restricted, and as long as they were mindful of the parameters he had laid down, he left them alone. Failure wasn't an option so he went about the business of life in England and set things in motion. His earliest venture into science fiction in the UK was as a producer of the *Armchair Theatre* episodes *I Can Destroy the Sun*, which aired on 12 October 1958 and starred Maurice Denham and Leslie Sands. The story revolves around a letter sent to British, American, and Soviet delegates at a nuclear disarmament convention, which reads rather cryptically "I can destroy the sun".

The Greatest Man in the World, which aired twenty-eight days later, starred Donald Pleasence and Patrick McGoohan who was later lead actor, and co-creator of the ITV series *The Prisoner* (1967-68). McGoohan plays Jack Smurch, an unknown American who builds a rocket and goes to the Moon, before being murdered by his own government. The story is set three years in the future, and opens with the state funeral for hero Jack Smurch. (Bareham, 2013) Hardly space stories at all, there are no special effects in either plays. *The Greatest Man* is made up of interviews with people being asked what they think of McGoohan's character Smurch. It is not about gadgetry, or robots, or flying saucers. If it had been necessary to show a rocket travelling through space Sydney would have asked the designers to make one, or used stock-footage – after all the space race was underway.

For the first time, technology had been rising up to meet the expectations of the science fiction writers, it was an exciting time. The two stories were a more subtle kind of science fiction focusing on the situation, but all of these experiences were helping Sydney, and came into play when planning *Target Luna*, which aired eighteen months later. Seen as a pre-cursor to *Doctor Who*, it was followed-up by *Pathfinders in Space*, *Pathfinders to Mars*, and *Pathfinders to Venus*.

One of ITV's earliest dramas written specifically for children, Sydney Newman's Pathfinders *series, has been described as the "missing link" between seminal BBC radio show* Journey Into Space *and* Doctor Who, *the latter of which Newman also created.*

Over three series broadcast during 1960 and 1961, the Pathfinders journeyed to the Moon and other worlds, facing drama at every turn – from space hazards to Venusian dinosaurs.

With intelligent and engaging scripts by Malcolm Hulke and Eric Paice, and a strong cast including actors Gerald Flood (Conway Henderson) and George Coulouris (Harcourt Brown), the series proved tremendously successful with the viewing public and even got into the regional top ten – unheard of for a children's programme. (Flint, 2013)

Chapter Eleven
Tapping a Vein

Twenty-one days after *The Greatest Man in the World* aired the ill-fated play *Underground* went out live, and the death of Gareth Jones shocked everyone. Only twenty-seven years old at the time, director Ted Kotcheff managed to keep a cool head and finish the show. Sydney and the rest of the crew were mortified, the thirty-three-year-old actor had been feeling unwell, but it was assumed he was just under the weather. There are a few versions of how he died exactly, with actor Peter Bowles saying it happened during the performance but it does appear his fatal heart-attack happened off-stage, and there was some mercy in the fact that it was quick. The audience noticed nothing during the performance, but for everyone else it was a truly terrifying time, and no amount of training or rehearsal could prepare a director for such an event. The newspapers carried obituaries for the Welshman and, as shocking as it was, Sydney and the crew had to get over it if the series was going to succeed, but Gareth's death was on everyone's mind for a long time. Another story suggests a vote was taken in the break to see if they should continue and that's why it wasn't taken off air. It didn't get much worse than this though, so what else was there for Sydney to fear?

The Boy with the Meat Axe aired on 23 November 1958, five years to the day before *Doctor Who* began. It was directed by Phillip Saville and starred a twenty-eight year old unknown actor called Sean Connery. Described as gritty and working-class, the play impressed most of the critics and saw a change of style in the series that shocked a lot of people.

"One must know who the audience is and, when dealing in millions, this is no easy thing. A tiny part of this mass audience who know something of the theatre, who have some knowledge of art, literature and history, would not be hard to please. When in doubt, give them Ibsen.

From the director's point of view, Ibsen is a piece of cake. He has seen his plays performed many times before. And of course, so have the critics. But this is academic because, in fact, I have to win and hold a vast audience from every walk of life and that is a far greater and more exciting challenge. To win approval without pandering to 'idiot' level is achievement enough for any man, particularly because the majority of this audience (12 million average) would never go to the theatre even if it were gratis with free beer in the intervals.

This vast audience may not have time to wait for Godot (no offence to Beckett), but those who would call them unintelligent on this count would be making a mistake. In fact, intelligence may have little to do with the enjoyment of a play. To satisfy the television audience may be a lot harder than to amuse pleasure-seeking and uncritical goers to a West End play. The theatre and cinema public, having made the effort to be parted with their money, become part of a captive audience. But the great TV audience is held by nothing but its own likes and dislikes. By the twist of a knob they can remove themselves from the 'theatre' without the embarrassment of a stumble over feet and a whispered "Excuse me!"

In one of our recent plays, owing to a flubby opening, 2,700,000 people from Land's End to John O'Groats, gave us 'the bird' by flicking off within the first seven minutes. No captive audience this!" (Newman[5], 1959)

Malcolm Hulke and Eric Paice's writing partnership kicked off in the summer of 1958 when their play *This Day in Fear* went out in the BBC's *Television* Playwright Series that aired between 1958 and 1959. They were then lured over to ABC, and wrote the *Armchair Theatre* episode *The Criminals* which aired on December 28. Hulke was hugely influential in the development of *Doctor Who* after its initial success, and

Armchair is where he first met Sydney. *The Criminals* was about a bank robbery, and in total Hulke and Paice wrote four episodes of the show before trying their hands at science-fiction on Sydney's shows *Target Luna,* and the three *Pathfinders* series. Hulke also wrote nine stories for *The Avengers,* either on his own, or with his friend Terrance Dicks who is one of a few people who can at least equal Malcolm's influence on *Doctor Who.* He was, however, also missing from the show's beginning and he became associated with the show in 1968. The first story Hulke wrote for *Doctor Who* was called *The Faceless Ones,* and starred Patrick Troughton. He wrote it with David Ellis in 1967, and by the time it aired Sydney was coming to the end of his time at the BBC, and shows he still had an influence on the series three years after Verity, and the original production team had left the series.

Hulke's association with *Doctor Who* goes back to season one, although his serial *Hidden Planet* was ultimately rejected after a dispute about disrupted payments. It would have been William Hartnell's seventh story, and was about a planet in an adjacent orbit to Earth where everything was opposite. By the time the dispute was over Carole Ann Ford had left the show, William Russell and Jacqueline Hill were about to do the same, and there was no time for a re-write. After Verity Lambert left near the end of 1965, and Patrick Troughton became the Doctor the following year, Hulke was finally pinned down to write *The Faceless Ones*. He was also responsible for adapting seven of the TV stories that were novelised by Target books, although Terrance Dicks wrote a staggering sixty-four, and cemented his name into a generation of young *Doctor Who* readers who had no real access to past-stories before video recorders became readily available.

The influence the two men have had on the show is massive, although Hulke died in 1979. Perhaps their biggest contribution was the co-creation of the Time Lords for Patrick Troughton's twelve-part regeneration epic *The War Games* in 1969, although it may have been producer Derrick Sherwin who first thought of the concept. Dicks became script-editor of the show in 1970, and stayed for the whole of Barry Letts' time as the show's producer. Hulke was also responsible for conceiving the idea of the the Silurians, and the Sea Devils whilst Dicks and Letts came up with The Master, all of which debuted during the reign of the third Doctor, Jon Pertwee. Having written all of the *Target Luna*, and the *Pathfinders* series' with Eric Paice it took Hulke three-and-a-half years to do a *Doctor Who* story, and his influence on the show certainly helped to shape the direction the show was going in, and colour TV was just around the corner.

The popularity of 'kitchen sink' drama and British music went hand in hand as 1958 rolled in 1959. In the summer, the BBC would put out its first edition of *Juke Box Jury*, and the Brit scene was influenced largely by American Rock 'n' Roll artists such as Elvis Presley and Jerry Lee Lewis until 1962 when beat music, and The Beatles came along. Teddy Boys were taking to the streets for the first time. At this time Alun Owen's playwriting skills were brought to Sydney's attention and his play *Progress to the Park*, in Stratford and in London, (Vahimagi, 2014) and was about four young men who pass into adulthood during one warm summer weekend in Liverpool. For Sydney, Owen crafted a story about three sailors just off a ship in Liverpool. *Called No Trams to Lime Street*, he assigned Ted Kotcheff to direct and the play became a success still talked of today. It is recognised as a cultural marker of change when the barriers between the classes, and what was right and wrong, began to change. The old ways were on their way out, and plays like Owen's showed people why instead of hiding it away.

No longer just a drama, Owen's play helped to turn *Armchair* into something people watched in their millions, it was one of the unmissable shows. For the first time, they were seeing the harsh realities of the world, their world, without the airs and graces, or having it told from the point of view of a Princess or a Baron. These were the people you saw in the street, down the market, in the pub, or outside the bookies puffing on Woodbines. The plays were giving a voice to the outrageous, the unaccepted, or the 'morally corrupt' as old attitudes were overturned. People were starting to wake up and realise that not everybody was the same, even if it was too early for society to accept ethnic minorities, or mothers giving birth out-of-wedlock at that point in time. *Armchair* was aired after the top-rated *Sunday Night at the London Palladium*, and the team took full advantage. At last, new writers were being found and developed, and the camera work and lighting was bold and new.

Buoyed by positive reviews and the self-confidence, Sydney came to the beginning of the most groundbreaking period of his career. His judgement, and his calculated risk taking, had mostly been sound so far, and this would continue. From the reinvention of *Armchair Theatre* in 1958, and the creation of cult shows such as *Police Surgeon*, *The Avengers*, *The Wednesday Play*, *Doctor Who*, and *Adam Adamant Lives!* From 'kitchen sink' Drama, to travellers in time and space, Sydney's ideas and influences in many genres must rank him alongside some of the greatest names in British TV, science fiction, and fantasy. It would be appropriate for his name to sit alongside such greats as Isaac Asimov, Arthur C. Clarke, George Lucas,

Terry Nation, Gene Roddenberry, Jules Verne and H. G. Wells, to name but a few. Most of these were writers and novelists, and Sydney's only recognised writing credits are early on in his career but his vision of what was realistic, as well as what he thought the future would hold, must rank him up there with those other greats. His ideas are still having an influence today, but we must not forget the role of Verity Lambert. It is for *Doctor Who* that Sydney gains much of this reputation, but there are other shows and policies he made that add to his importance. His obituary in *The Guardian* Newspaper called him the most important Impresario in Britain during his time over here, and today the *Doctor Who* brand is at least as big as top American science fiction franchises such as *Star Trek* and *Star Wars*, although Sydney's name has never appeared in the shows credits – as the Head of Drama at the BBC it wasn't the done thing as he would have been responsible for hundreds of shows. A fitting tribute would be to see both Sydney and Verity acknowledged in the modern-day version of the show, and this has been suggested by the *Doctor Who*'s first director, Waris Hussein.

As proud as Sydney was of *Doctor Who*, he admits it was just one show he had to oversee. When Hartnell left, and they were looking for the second Doctor, he suggested the idea of a cosmic-hobo type character, but by this time he was nearing the end of his time at the BBC. The production team knew what he was looking for, and if they got it wrong he was the one who carried the can, but he continued to let the popularity of the show do the talking. He was usually on hand to visit sets and see what was happening when needed, or offer ideas and advice if he thought it necessary, but he knew what it was like having somebody sitting on your shoulder when you were trying to work – he'd quit jobs over it in the past. Of course, there had to be limitations on creativity, a fine line needed to be trod because bringing *Doctor Who* to life was a rather intricate task. If Sydney had insisted on the Hulke / Paice writing team penning the opening stories of series one the show would have been very different, but in Verity, Sydney saw a shining-light who had the intelligence to protect herself from the baying wolves of the BBC old-guard. An indication of the type of man Sydney was comes from him going on record and admitting his mistakes. His approach was not autocratic, and he allowed Verity Lambert the freedom she enjoyed even though he didn't always agree with her way of doing things. He never wanted Susan to be the Doctor's granddaughter, and if he'd had his wish there would certainly have been an enhanced aired of mystery surrounding the show. Why would a beautiful young girl be travelling through time and space with a man with no name?

Others shows that forged Sydney's reputation include *The Avengers*, and *The Forsyte Saga* in 1967, and 'kitchen sink' drama is still around today and is a far more diverse genre. Tony Warren was one of the early writers to capitalise, and he had a big success with *Coronation Street*, even though modern audiences have become desensitised to much of what was counted as drama in the 1950s and 60s. A passionate kiss, a flash of thigh, or a televised murder on the TV set at 8pm is now run-of-the-mill. Soap-Opera is far more graphic, and modern writers aren't hindered by the degree of censorship around in Sydney's day, which isn't necessarily a good thing. Soaps are highly-exaggerated, and can be an overwhelmingly depressing version of real-life which begs the question – do people see too much negativity in shows like *Eastenders*, *Hollyoaks*, and *Coronation Street*? To what capacity do we subconsciously imitate the behaviours we see in these twisted versions of reality or are we smarter than that? Many of the science fiction franchises offer hope for the future, or of a Utopia where humanity lives in peace with nature and science. Sydney would have wanted such concepts to poke through the gritty realism and give the viewer a glimpse of an alternative path towards a brighter future, although he showed people the dirt and the grime too. *Armchair Theatre* was a phenomenal success for Sydney and his team, but it wasn't always 'kitchen sink' from then on in. They tried to mix it around a bit, there were also comedies and science fiction, murder-thriller and love stories before a hard-hitting social drama was aired. They used all the different types of people in society, from Doctors and Scientists, to factory-workers and criminals. Everyone could relate to what they saw on screen.

Chapter Twelve
Armchair Avenger

The Avengers grew out of *Police Surgeon* which Sydney had commissioned and it subsequently failed. It aired from September to December 1960, and it showed that the star, Ian Hendry, was both photogenic and versatile, and was the kind of actor who could captivate the audience with his all-action style. He'd served his National Service after the war with the 32nd Medium Regiment, Royal Army. During this time, he was also a very keen athlete, and he ran a motorcycle stunt team so he had to be fit, and had kept up that regime. Howard Thomas had suggested to Sydney that ABC could do with a thriller and this got him thinking out the idea for the show, and he thought that Hendry could go on to greater things. As it would be with *Doctor Who*, it was the role of his producers and directors to move the concept of *The Avengers* into reality, and of the name, Sydney once remarked that he didn't know what it meant.

Selecting Ian Hendry to play Doctor David Keel was not so much a choice as an inheritance. Indeed, he was virtually reprising his role of Doctor Geoffrey Brent from the half-hour crime drama Police Surgeon. *Incidentally, one of the reasons Hendry was given a partner in* The Avengers *is that it was felt he could not carry a full hour of drama alone. The role of the spy, John Steed, went to Patrick Macnee...*

The original secret agent side-kick might have been inspired by Philip John Stead, a British secret agent during WWII, who was a codes and security expert. By the time The Avengers *was on the air, he had retired into academia. He became an expert on police systems and an author... It is uncertain if Philip John Stead was indeed the inspiration for Sydney Newman's character, John Steed, or if it was all just a strange coincidence...*

It was September 1960 when, out of the blue, producer Leonard White, a friend of Macnee's from his years in Canada, suggested he see Sydney Newman about an acting part in a new TV series. Unwilling to return to acting (or, more to the point, return to an actor's wage), Macnee almost rejected the offer. But when White pointed out that Macnee had done nothing in the two years since he produced The Valiant Years, *Macnee found it difficult to argue.*

Macnee agreed to do the part, but when Newman balked at Macnee's requested salary (£150 per week, as opposed to per episode, the latter being bi-weekly), Macnee apparently "blackmailed" him into the higher figure by making reference to an unsavoury event in Montreal involving Newman and another director. More than that is not known presently. (Keel, 2002)

Sydney's hunch that Hendry would go onto greater things was correct, and after one series he left to pursue a film-career, and appeared in films such as *Get Carter*, *The Bitch*, and *McVicar*. McNee's character was eventually teamed up with a female sidekick Cathy Gale who was played by Honor Blackman, and the show became even more of a hit. It ran for seven seasons in total. The first episode *Hot Snow* aired on 18 March 1962 and was produced by Leonard White. It was also hit badly by the policy of wiping videotape in the 1960s and only a few episodes remain from the first series, with around 20 minute of the first hour-long episode existing. The first *Doctor Who* writer to be involved was Dennis Spooner who penned episode six *Girl On the Trapeze*, but Peter Ling, John Lucarotti, and Bill Strutton all wrote episodes for the first series. Like *Doctor Who*, *The Avengers* changed significantly as the years went by, with new side-kicks coming and going, and even the genre being modified from spy-thriller to fantasy – it even dipped its toes in the realms of science fiction. The show continued until May 1969 and the later seasons were shot on film so it looked more like a James Bond movie which made it more saleable abroad. It was resurrected in 1976 as The New Avengers which ran for two seasons, and in recent years there has been a Hollywood version starring Uma Thurman. Although the original shows have gained cult-status and become a world-wide success, the Hollywood version flopped at the box office. At the very start the show could have so easily have gone that way – after Henry left they were unsure if people would still watch.

Newman again turned to the production team and asked them to create a new character to co-star with Patrick Macnee. He toyed with the idea of getting in a woman to partner Steed, thinking that this might create a new dynamic. In the end they went for three different partners: a male medic, Dr King (Jon Rollason), a chirpy nightclub singer, Venus Smith (Julie Stevens) and a leather-clad renaissance woman, Cathy Gale (Honor Blackman).

They used the scripts that had been intended for Macnee and Hendry so often that Cathy Gale would find herself in situations written for a male, dealing with villains with judo and fisticuffs. The result caused a sensation. The third series partnered Steed and Gale full-time and when (Leonard) White left the series midway through that third season, it was in robust health.

At the same time, White was also running the ITV sci-fi anthology series, Out of This World... *At the end of 1962, unhappy with the decision to make* Armchair Theatre *fortnightly, Sydney Newman abruptly left ABC to become Head of Drama at the BBC.* (Fiddy, 2016)

Fiddy (2016), as just stated, said that Sydney left because he was unhappy with ABC's decision to cut *Armchair Theatre* to a two-weekly series, and it was only later that *The Avengers* became a global phenomenon, and the same thing happened with *Doctor Who*. Although it was big in Britain when he was the head of drama at the BBC, it was virtually unheard of in the USA and other countries. It is also interesting to note that *The Avengers* went out later in America because it was considered violent. The 1960s were to be one of the busiest times in Sydney's career with his dual role as Head of Drama, and as a producer. *Armchair* wasn't the only show he was working on – he produced three new shows, and three spin offs for ABC in 1960. *Counter-Attack* began in January and lasted for seven episodes, and *Inside Story* started in February. *Target Luna* blasted-off in April, and with the three spin-off *Pathfinders* series' the whole run went on into 1961. He also produced twenty-four *Armchair Theatre* shows, and all of this was before he put on his hat and became the boss.

By 1962, things were changing at ABC despite Sydney being heralded a success as both Head of Drama, and as a producer. He had brought a Canadian influence to ABC, although he wasn't the first to do so. Ted Kotcheff had been directing in England before he arrived, and he was instrumental in Sydney's decision to come over and work. 'Kitchen-sink' drama had evolved too – there were now more freedoms, youngsters, women and ethnic minorities now had a voice as people pushed for equality and freedom. All the while the poets, writers, artists and composers listened and watched all of this unfolding before them and, with minds-ablaze, they went to work. In the creative industry technologies and methods were changing fast and making the creative process easier which meant program-making soared to new heights.

In February, Alvin Rakoff directed an episode of *Armchair, written by Rod Serling,* called *The Strike* which was re-titled *Come in Razor Red* because of the meaning of the word in Britain. In America, Rod Serling had created *The Twilight Zone* in 1959 which was a weekly collection of unconnected stories that were usually psychological thrillers, science fiction, or fantasies with an unexpected twist towards the end. *Razor Red* saw Richard Harris playing a tough commander contemplating whether he should order an airstrike to destroy the enemy. He knows that it will kill him and his troops, and has to weigh up the choices. (Sellers, 2012) Season three of *Armchair* was a mammoth affair for all involved and Serling's story was well received. The whole season ran for eighteen months, and in total there were eighty-nine episodes. The success of the show really helped to put Sydney on the map.

The Beatles would have fit right into Alun Owen's *No Trams to Lime Street* which aired in 1959, and popularised the Liverpudlian accent on television three years before their TV debut in October 1962. They had spent the summer recording at Abbey Road Studios for the first time and released their debut single *Love Me Do* at the end of the year, but the idea of working-class heroes was already in people's psyches before they arrived on the scene. In America, there were icons like James Dean and Elvis Presley, it was the music and the look that every teen wanted. At cinemas and clubs, fairgrounds and dances, the barriers of the old traditions were breaking down in Britain and Sydney played his part in that process. At the very least he gave a voice to those who were making the moves with the freedom he allowed himself and his writers and directors. The Brits were taking back control of their language and culture, and all eyes began to refocus on the country that had been battered by the ravages of war. Now there was a new beat, and new ways of thinking, and if you were a writer or a filmmaker you had to get amongst it, and London was the place to be.

The *Armchair Theatre* shows kept coming thick and fast, *His Polyvinyl Girl* was about a man who falls in love with a department store mannequin that comes to life at night, and Robert Holmes (creator of the Autons) was also working for ITV when the play aired. He worked on shows such as *Ghost Squad*, *Knight Errant* and *Emergency-Ward 10* for ATV, and is another key figure in the history of *Doctor Who*. He said that his idea of living plastic and shop-mannequins springing to life came to him after watching an episode of Kit Pedler and Gerry Davis's show *Doomwatch* (which ran from 1970 to 1972). The first episode of *Doomwatch*, *The Plastic Eaters*, is about a man-made virus with the power to eat all plastic, but it aired a month after Holmes' creation The Autons made their first appearance in the *Doctor Who* story *Spearhead From Space* in January 1970. Whether Holmes had access to the scripts for *The Plastic Eaters* before the show went out is unknown, as is the influence of *Polyvinyl Girl* on his creation. What is known is that many of *Doctor Who*'s early cast and crew worked in the same circles, and on the same shows, and they would have talked and been influenced by one another. *The Avengers* used scripts written by *Doctor Who* dignitaries such as Terry Nation, Malcolm Hulke, Dennis Spooner and Terrance Dicks, and they were all part of the creative hive of people who worked on everything from *Stingray* to *Hancock*. John Gosling and Anthony Kearney's *Ghost Squad* (1961-64) used writers Anthony Coburn, Robert Banks Stewart, John Lucarotti and actors Roger Delgado and William Hartnell. Producers and directors were making associations all the time, and the seed of the idea for the man in the box travelling through time and space was rattling around in Sydney's head with a hundred other ideas at that point in time. After *Pathfinders*, he would have had the confidence to undertake such a project, but would need to jump ship to the BBC before that idea could be pinned down and made into reality.

'Beatlemania' was on its way, and so was Sydney. The sounds of the era were *Telstar* by The Tornadoes, Little Eva's *The Loco-Motion*, and *The Young Ones* by Cliff Richard. On television in 1962, there were debuts for *Z Cars* and *Steptoe and Son* on the BBC, and *The Saint* and *Police 5* on ITV. In October, just four years after appearing on *Armchair Theatre* as a virtual unknown, Sean Connery starred as James Bond in the first film, *Dr No,* of the long running series. England, and in particular London, was certainly the place to be and Sydney was in the thick of it – literally. A choking smog was not uncommon at the time, and of course the place was a lot busier than Toronto, but he loved his time in the city. He had of course experienced life in New York City for a year with his family, but England was quite different, and was steeped in mystery. Despite his fondness for the UK he would eventually return to Canada. There was no question of him staying in England permanently, or even settling in Hollywood – he had offers from studios throughout his career. At the end of the day he was Canadian, and his heart would always be with the country of his birth.

Mary Whitehouse went on to set up the National Viewers and Listeners Association in 1965 to oppose what she saw as obscenity on television and radio. Nobody could deny the fact there were unmarried mothers, alcoholics, drug-addicts and rough sleepers in Britain, but Whitehouse and her followers believed their plight shouldn't disturb Sunday evening viewing after they'd already done their bit in church that day. In the Pink Floyd song, *Time* from 1973, there's a line which says 'Hanging on in quiet desperation is the English way' and nothing sums up better how those on the margins of society felt in Britain at the time. With little help and no jobs, the death of so many great industries had made things even tougher after the war. There was an idea that people should get on with it though, no matter how bad it was, but in truth there was nothing wrong with holding out a hand for help. Charitable organisations were set up to do just that, surely these people deserved a voice as much as a hot meal and somewhere to sleep? Sydney certainly believed so. *Armchair Theatre*, and later *The Wednesday Play*, tried to educate as well as prick the consciences of those in better positions, but by 1962 (and realising they didn't want to flog a dead-horse) he was only interested in making 'kitchen sink' drama if it was exceptional. They had covered so much by then they had to be careful not to repeat themselves and drive viewers away.

The *Armchair Theatre* episode *The Man Out There* by Donald Giltinan aired on March 12 1961, and starred Patrick McGoohan whose rocket becomes faulty and he gets trapped in space. Sydney produced it, and Charles Jarrott was the director – and a month after it was shown Russian cosmonaut Yuri Gagarin became the first man in space. After the launch of Sputnik in 1957, it became obvious to everyone that a man would soon be sent up, and that the subject was of huge interest to the general public. *Armchair Theatre* was flexible enough to be able to respond to what was happening on so many levels, and *The Man Out There* tapped into feelings and emotions hidden away by society, or not fully realised. It could also respond to what was in the news, and what people in the pubs and clubs were talking about, and appear as if the shows were almost telling the future – as is the case in this story. Week-after-week they were stealing viewers from the other channel and attracting huge audiences.

*It was this series (*Armchair Theatre*) that made the director-general (of the BBC) instruct Kenneth Adam to try and get Sydney Newman because of what I had done, my plays were highly entertaining and gripping, but the fact is they did have a very serious content. They were about the times, they were about live issues, they were what people subconsciously needed and wanted...*

Kenneth Adam said "would you like to join the BBC?", and I said "what have you in mind?" And he said "To take over our Sunday Night play" and I laughed. I said "You're joking, why should I walk across the street to do precisely what I'm doing in Armchair Theatre?*" We talked about that, and he said "Would you like to be head of our drama?" I said, "Now you're talking".* (Newman[3], 1966)

Armchair Theatre had often dipped its toes into science fiction, and it had not gone unnoticed. Irene Shubik was a script-editor on the show, and she suggested to Sydney that they make a science fiction version. Born in London, Shubik had been evacuated to Canada during the war. She had moved in similar circles to Sydney and he liked her. What's more, he liked the idea. The show they made was called *Out Of This World*, and it was a thirteen-part series that aired in June 1962. Each episode was hosted by Boris Karloff, and were plays that were written by famous science fiction writers such as Isaac Asimov and Philip K. Dick. Sydney was involved in the production of one of the episodes, but it was Leonard White who was the overseer. Other names involved with the show, and later with *Doctor Who*, included Terry Nation, Jacqueline Hill, and Philip Madoc, and the series dealt with everything from stowaways on rocket-ships, to conjurers' boxes that people went into and never returned. By the time it aired, Sydney was waiting for his contract to end so he could join the BBC. He'd asked ABC if he could leave early but they were not pleased, and they made him stay to very near the end. By this time the newspapers were calling him a prisoner at Teddington studios, and it was an unpleasant end for what had otherwise been a successful and happy time.

Chapter Thirteen
Visiting Aunty

On April 26, 1962 *The Stage* reported that Sydney had joined the BBC, but of course he couldn't take up the offer until the end of the year as he was still under contract with ABC.

The BBC were paying him top money, but it was still £3,000 less than he was getting at ABC. Still, the chance to be involved in overseeing 720 programs a year, and a budget reported to be around ten million pounds, was too good an offer to refuse. (Falk, 1974) As Sydney said on many occasions, life was not always about money – although the BBC salary was still generous, it just wasn't as much as his former employers had paid him. Long gone were the days of scratching a living as an artist, now he was moving with the shakers in British society, and he'd overcome a good deal of racism and discrimination to get there. Some saw him as the 'Loud Mouthed Yank' despite being Canadian, but the truth was he didn't really care what they thought. He had such a strong belief in what he was doing, and he was about to put the biggest rocket up the posteriors of the old-guard at the BBC as he rung the changes. They weren't keen on outsiders but Sydney didn't care. If they weren't going to accept him and move with the times, then they were out the door.

Arriving at Wood Lane just in time to see the 1962 Christmas programming, Sydney was given an office on the fifth floor which was also where his staff were, so he was in amongst them from the start. He stood out because he usually wore a tweed suit and a bow-tie, and of course there was his accent. Some would have felt threatened by him, but there were also those who embraced his individualism. Director Don Taylor was one of Sydney's strongest critics and he was soon shown the door. It was a difficult job, and he wouldn't pick it up overnight. He soon realised the BBC was a lot different to ITV, they had stricter standards and a bigger reputation to uphold and Sydney began to quickly see the differences. Over the Christmas the scheduling was hectic, and he arrived in the thick of it and had to hit the ground running. Some of the TV highlights that year were: *Christmas Crackerjack* with Eamonn Andrews, Johnny Morris' *Tales of the Riverbank*, *Benny Hill* and *Z Cars* which all drew big viewing figures, as did *Billy Smart's Circus*.

Sydney knew the job wouldn't be easy, and some of the heavyweight executives he had around him such as Donald Baverstock, Michael Peacock, and Huw Wheldon didn't like failure, although the atmosphere wasn't oppressive. He had proved in the past that he couldn't work in such an environment, and he wouldn't have stayed if it had been that way, no matter how big the reputation of the BBC. There was pressure on Sydney, but he coped well with it. He put in the hours and the effort and left nothing to chance. If he did fail he could always tuck his tail between his legs and run off back to Canada. What was apparent from the off was that the drama department was crying out for change, and new talent was sought. The organisation had fallen some way behind ITV who had lots of great shows.

In March 1963, Chief of Programmes Donald Baverstock made Newman aware of a need for a series to bridge the gap between sports showcase Grandstand *and pop music programme* Juke Box Jury *on Saturday evenings. Newman considered a variety of ideas, including a show about two boys at a boarding school, before finally deciding on one of his favourite genres: science fiction. He asked Wilson to develop an idea for a 52-week series, which would be made up of shorter individual serials.*
On March 26th, Wilson convened a meeting with John Braybon, Alice Frick and C. E. (Cecil Edwin) "Bunny"

Webber, also of the Script Department. The result was an idea for a series called The Troubleshooters, *about a group of three scientific consultants: a "handsome young man hero", a "handsome well-dressed heroine aged about 30" and a "maturer man, 35-40, with some 'character' twist".*

Newman was not thrilled by the proposal. He particularly disagreed with the decision to avoid using a younger character, feeling that a teenager would be ideal to help embroil the other protagonists in their adventures. Newman did concur with the suggestion that the programme might involve the use of a time machine, and it was he who came up with the idea that this ship could be bigger on the inside than on the outside. Newman also found great inspiration in the character of the "maturer man". Eschewing the suggested age, Newman developed a frail, grumpy old man called the Doctor who has stolen the time machine from his own alien people.

Sydney communicated his thoughts back to Wilson, who helped Sydney to reorganise the Drama Department, and was given the job of Head of Serials. It was hoped that the first episode of the new series could be ready for recording (on videotape) on July 5 at Lime Grove Studio D in London; and film sequences would be completed at the Ealing Television Film Studios the week before. The debut transmission would follow on Saturday, July 27.

In May, BBC veteran Rex Tucker was brought in to serve as producer pending a permanent appointment. Tucker had gotten his start as a writer for children's radio programmes, later moving to children's television in the Fifties. He worked for the BBC as a writer, director and producer, with credits including a variety of classics serials. It was therefore also thought that Tucker would direct the new programme's first serial. (Sullivan, 2016)

Alongside *The Avengers* and *Armchair Theatre*, ITV had a new soap-opera called *Coronation Street* which knocked the spots off BBC's *Compact* which went out on Tuesday and Thursday evenings to avoid clashing with *Coronation Street* on Monday and Wednesday. ITV also had other great shows like *Danger Man*, and *Top Secret*, and Sydney knew that it was going to take a lot of effort for the BBC to get back on top. A bit of thinking outside the box needed to be done, and for this ability Sydney was the answer to the BBC's prayers - although there were still those who voiced their displeasure at his appointment. In the past, the organisation hadn't worried about audience figures, but all of that had changed - as had the technology – so Sydney had to make sweeping changes until he had what he wanted, and he had to be ruthless.

We make programs for people. We don't plan our programs on costs per thousand basis... the ordinary Joe, and I include myself in that, we want all things. I want to laugh to Beverley Hillbillies, *and I want to think, and I want to be made to cry. I want to be made to laugh, and all these things comes from the total diet of television fair, if the fair is properly balanced.* (Newman[3], 1966)

In the early 1960s, it became easier to record and edit shows which were later sold abroad, but many episodes from this era were wiped so that the tape could be used again – such was its cost. In hindsight, we can see how much of a tragedy this is, but nobody foresaw it at the time, or the fact one day that episodes or an entire series would be sold so that people could watch privately at home. If they had seen the historical importance of keeping material maybe a budget for preservation, and the storage of videotape, would have been made available, but from today's perspective such junking appears extremely short-sighted. Video recorders didn't become common-place in homes until the early 1980s, and at the time of writing 97 episodes of *Doctor Who* are still missing. The BBC didn't have an archiving policy in place until the late 1970s, so much of the output from before then has been lost. Sydney's other important creation at the BBC, *The Wednesday Play* is still regarded as one of the most important shows of the 1960s, and only 76 of the 127 episodes survive today. Almost all of the studio coverage of the Apollo Moon landing was junked, as were episodes of *Not Only But Also*, *Dixon of Dock Green*, *Dads Army*, *Sykes*, *Steptoe & Son*, and *Z-Cars* to name but a few. Occasionally episodes of *Doctor Who* are found abroad or in obscure places, and at the time of writing the last discovery was in Nigeria in 2013. Fortunately, audio-recordings and tele-snaps of lost episodes are still in existence, although some are in poor condition.

In the 1950s, the BBC set up the Visual Effects Department, and the Radiophonic Workshop whose initial remit was to produce sound-effects for radio. By 1960, many of the pieces were in place to produce a science fiction series. In 1962, Alice Frick and Donald Bull (from the BBC's survey group) were commissioned to write a report that looked into the viability of making such a programme, but they didn't reach any real conclusions. Frick then worked with John Braybon on a second report and all their findings were sent to Donald Wilson, the Head of the script department who became Head of Serials after Sydney shut the script department down. Wilson was responsible for overseeing the development of the new show, and he reported directly to Sydney who was busy formulating his own ideas. Many things would have influenced him as he sat down and wrote out his idea for *Doctor Who*, and the BBC reports were certainly influential.

In the report the authors discussed the idea of travelling through time and space in a negative manner, but Sydney didn't agree, what's more he'd known how to do it since he'd read *The Time Machine* as a boy. Fresh in his mind was George Pal's 1960 film adaption starring Rod Taylor which tells the story of the time-traveller George who has the whole of history to explore, and ends up in the far-future helping enslaved humanity. There had never been such a diverse format as this, and Sydney knew it. A time-traveller could find himself in any situation that the writer could dream-up, and such a show had the potential to run for at least fifty-two weeks. The idea of the time-machine being bigger inside than out was a stroke of genius, but only once did they film an entire show inside the machine during the original series. It was called *The Edge of Destruction*, broadcast in 1964, and was penned by *Compact* writer David Whitaker David Whitaker, who was also script editor of the show. He wrote it because Chief of Programmes Donald Baverstock was concerned about the projected costs of the show and didn't want it to continue beyond the first story. Sydney and Donald Wilson managed to convince him to continue, and the two-part story was written to show the strengths of the show even when confined to a small space. It was equally important to show Baverstock how cheaply the show could be made.

Sydney's emphasis was on making serials, but the problem was encapsulating realistic action and drama before a television camera. By using clever tricks such as realistic scenery and lighting great things were achieved, although often this wasn't always the case. This was the beginning of a golden era for BBC drama, and after a while Sydney began to pull the strings together which would result in the original outline for *Doctor Who*.

Frick and Bull's first report highlighted the dominance of America in the science fiction genre. It also suggested it wasn't a particularly popular branch of fiction so, special attention would need to be taken to create the right kind of show. The second report proved to be more precise, and it outlined stories by authors such as Poul Anderson and Eric Frank Russell after the first failed to identify any science fiction writers. It also suggested that all serials should be written by TV dramatists who had a better grasp of what audiences wanted. It also agreed with the use of time-travel, and by this time Sydney was already taken with the idea. It wasn't just *The Time Machine* that popularised the theme, there were also the films *Beyond the*

Time Barrier and *La Jetée* around at that time, as well as the novels *The End of Eternity* by Isaac Asimov, and *The Time Traders* by Andre Norton, and Sydney knew the idea could work.

Between 1953 and 1958, the BBC produced three Quatermass science-fiction mini-series written by Nigel Kneale which proved to be extremely popular. Future *Doctor Who* luminaries Paddy Russell, Roger Delgado, John Scott Martin, and Dick Mills were involved in some of the shows which were based on the activities of Professor Bernard Quatermass and the British Space Programme. Despite its popularity, Sydney knew science fiction could be done better, and he also realised that the output of the BBC drama department could be vastly improved. A lot of things needed an overhaul, including the staff, many of them had been with the corporation for years and were now part of the furniture. He suggested the drama department needed a "good kick", and that is when he split it into three separate units (Plays, Series, and Serials) so each could concentrate on different types of productions.

There was a perception that BBC Drama was just radio with pictures, and now with commercial pressures upon them, he had the power to make changes. It was hard enough to make *Doctor Who* in 1963, and a show as technical as it was could never have been made ten years earlier when they were making *Quatermass*. Sydney wanted his dramas to break away from tradition, although *Doctor Who* didn't often benefit from revolutionary technology, or from an increased budget. In the beginning, the production was allocated £2,300 per episode, which is around £34,000 in 2017, and the budget for the TARDIS was just £500. They were expecting miracles on a shoe-string budget, and it's true to say it didn't always work. It was good enough to capture people's imaginations though, although this meant the actors and the crew had to work flat-out with every ounce of energy and resource they had to make the show feel convincing.

When *Doctor Who* began it was just another children's show that may not have lasted very much past Christmas 1963. Today the money it generates and its longevity make it very much a flagship for the BBC. After disbanding the children's department in 1963, Sydney charged the drama department with making shows aimed at younger viewers, and in March, a meeting took place with the Controller of Programmes Donald Baverstock, and Assistant Controller Joanna Spicer to discuss the Saturday night problem which they wanted Sydney to do something about because they were losing out as people were switching over to the other side.

"In between was a children's classic serial, Dickens etcetera, and the audience was tremendous for sports. Then, there'd be a big dip, and then they'd start building again at a quarter-to-six (For Juke Box Jury*). So, I was asked by Baverstock, and this emerged in the program review meetings, could I dream up some kind of drama that would appeal to children, and would be lively and so on"* (Newman[2], 2006)

Chapter Fourteen
Mister Who? Doctor X?

On March 26 1963, Donald Wilson held a meeting to discuss the new science fiction show, and Alice Frick and John Braybon were in attendance, as well as a Cecil "Bunny" Webber, a writer from the defunct script department. From this meeting came another report credited as being key to the beginnings of *Doctor Who*, and it certainly pulled together ideas floating around at the time. It was written by Webber for Sydney, was titled, *"Dr Who: General notes on Background and Approach"* and was the first time all these elements were formulated under the heading of *"Dr Who"*. One of the most striking differences to the television format are the names of the characters, Bridget, Miss McGovern, and Cliff, who became Susan Foreman, Barbara Wright, and Ian Chesterton. Much of the memo formalises and expands upon Sydney's original idea, although the Doctor character was fine-tuned even further, and Hartnell eventually played him how Sydney wanted after he ordered a re-shoot of the original pilot episode. This was an extremely rare thing to do because of the cost involved, but

Sydney wasn't convinced by the original performance. He asked Hartnell to play the Doctor in a more likeable way – in the original he had been too mean and Sydney didn't want *Doctor Who* going the way of *Mr X*. The ideas the designers came up with for the show were outstanding, and he knew if they could get everything right it wouldn't become the expensive albatross many of his critics were praying for. He may have felt differently if he had read Terry Nation's script *The Mutants* – the writer himself admits to not wanting to do it, and he initially turned *Doctor Who* down. When he fell out with Tony Handcock he found himself short of work so the intention was to knock-out *Doctor Who* scripts quickly to make some money. Nation then began writing for Eric Sykes and forgot all about the script, which became *The Daleks*, until it was big news.

The Daleks has been attributed as the show's catalyst, making it successful and has certainly made a big contribution to its longevity. The importance of Hartnell's performance is sometimes underestimated, after all, the amazing creatures, planets and machines are but accompaniments to him. The show is called *Doctor Who* because its primary concern is a character of unknown origins that Sydney dreamed-up. By linking his interests in art and the human condition, to science fiction and an out-of-date puppet-show he came up with a compelling character full of mystery and alien intelligence who has the whole of time and space at his disposal. He also has some affinity to the Earth, which begs the question why is he here at the start of the first episode? Is it because he is half-human as stated in the 1996 *Doctor Who Movie*? The Doctor was originally conceived to be an alien scientist and a grandfather in Edwardian attire. The re-shoot dealt with a number of technical issues Sydney had observed during the original episode, and after that they were good to go again.

It has been necessary to provide evidence of Sydney's thinking, and the people and events that inspired him, as an evolutionary process throughout this book because his original thoughts on *Doctor Who* stretch far back. Webber's memo shows that the creation of the show was a team effort, and there is so much crossing-over of ideas it is extremely difficult to pinpoint exactly who created what. We must be careful here if history is going to do justice to the man who started the whole thing off. We must remember there is no evidence of Sydney collaborating on the original idea until it became 'a show' and went into the planning stage and became *Doctor Who*. We have seen that the seeds of the idea had been with him for at least fifteen years, and his recall of why and how he created it acknowledged the role of the others who were involved.

Doctor Who was really the culmination of almost all my interests in life: I wanted to reflect contemporary society; I was curious about the outer-space stuff; and also, of course, being a children's programme, it had to have a high educational content. Up to the age of forty, I don't think there was a science fiction book I hadn't read. I love them because they're a marvellous way – a safe way – of saying nasty things about our own society. I'd read H. G. Wells, of course, and I recalled his book 'The Time Machine'. That inspired me to dream up the time-space machine for 'Doctor Who'. It was a great device which allowed my audience to be taken to outer space, to elsewhere in the world today, or back into the past.

I then dreamed up this senile old man of 740 years of age to be the running character. He has fled in terror from another planet in this spaceship which lands on Earth in the form of a police box. He's wandering around in the London fog when he's met by two school teachers who are walking home one of their pupils. They help him to what they think is his house, but it's a police telephone box in a junkyard! But inside, it's really a vast spaceship! However, this dim old guy doesn't know how to operate the machine, presses the wrong button and they take off. And that was the idea.

Donald Wilson thought it was 'possibly' a good idea. Although a Scot, he was frightfully English – very correct, pipe-smoking, everything but a handkerchief in his sleeve! He was very cautious and wouldn't commit himself. I loved that man, because he was so different from me. He was very cultured, tall and lean; and he was always amused by me, because I was so crude.

I remembered this extremely bright girl called Verity Lambert, who had worked for me as a production assistant at ABC. I called her up and said "D'you want to be a producer?" She was only a personal assistant and said "Of course!" I gave her a two-page memo on 'Doctor Who' and said "Can you do it?". She said "Yeah, okay" and she did! I'd give a million bucks if someone could find that memo.

Verity was the one who realised it all, although I had a hand in the casting. I helped her quite a bit in the beginning, because she was inexperienced as a producer, and she was frightened to death coming to the BBC. However, she had worked with some of my best directors – like Ted Kotcheff and Philip Saville – so she knew the production grass roots extremely well. And she turned out to be a real winner. I'm told there were quite a few rumblings within the BBC, because she'd never been a director, and because she was a girl. She was tough, good-looking and stubborn. If she didn't like something, she came out honestly and said so. It wasn't "I don't know why I don't like this", it was "I don't like it because of X, Y and Z, it should be A, B and C". She was very positive, as a good producer has to be.

We shot a dummy run and it didn't work out right because Bill Hartnell's characterisation was a bit too nasty and I thought he'd put off the viewers. Also, I wanted one character with whom my children's audience could identity, and who was a stranger to Dr. Who, but somehow it turned out that Dr. Who was her grandfather. And I never wanted that – ever! I've never forgiven Verity for that!

With the educational aspect in mind, I wrote in my memo that the outer space stories must be based on factual knowledge about outer space. Also, by going back in time we could bring history alive for the young, having 'Doctor Who' and his earthlings on the shores of Britain when Caesar landed – that sort of situation. Being a real aficionado of science fiction, I hated stories which used bug-eyed monsters, otherwise known as BEM's. I wrote in my memo that there would be no bug-eyed monsters in 'Doctor Who'. And after a few episodes, Verity turned up with the Daleks! I bawled her out for it, but she said "Honest, Sydney, they're not bug-eyed monsters – they're human beings who are so advanced that their bodies have atrophied and they need these casings to manipulate and do the things they want!" Of course, the Daleks took off and captured everybody's imagination. Some of the best things I have ever done are the things I never wanted to do. It's true! It's worked out that way . (Newman[6], 1986)

The characters supporting the Doctor in the show were also 'fleshed out' further after their names were changed, and Sydney's instructions, although not detailed, were largely adhered to:

These are the characters we know and sympathise with, the ordinary people to whom extraordinary things happen. The fourth basic character remains always something of a mystery, and is seen by us rather through the eyes of the other three. (Newman[4], 1963)

Not only was Verity the youngest ever producer at the BBC at twenty-seven, she was the only female in that position, although she wasn't the first female as is a common misconception, and close support was provided by the experienced Mervyn Pinfield in an associate-producer role. Born in London in 1935, Roedean educated Verity began working for ITV in 1956. She started out as a secretary at Granada television, and then at ABC after she was dismissed, and her rapid rise to BBC producer took only seven years. Moving into production after a short while at ABC, she got her break on *Armchair Theatre* under Sydney, but left ABC in 1961 to work in America for 12 months as a personal assistant to producer and TV host David Susskind. When she returned to ABC she had the desire to direct, and gave herself a year to do it or she vowed to quit television. Sydney was the kind of man who liked to take a chance when he saw potential, although he admitted she was not his first choice for *Doctor Who*. What he did know was she was made of the right kind of stuff to cope with the job which he called: 'Piss and Vinegar', and he remembered how she'd kept her cool on the live episode of *Armchair Theatre* when Gareth Jones died. Apart from this Sydney saw potential, and when she took the job on *Doctor Who* she had a great deal of sexism to overcome. Without her the show would not have gone on to become the institution it is today. Many people have been a big influence on its development, but Verity was the one who brought Sydney's idea to life.

Sydney was not a writer, he was an ideas man with a good eye as an overseer, although he did author scripts and direct. Verity was the next link in the chain, and once concepts were laid down they began to think about scripts, locations, budget, and how they were going to make it work. Director Richard Martin was responsible for twenty-two episodes, and he states the show's name came from when Sydney was prompted in a meeting with director Rex Tucker. *Doctor Who* was the name that stuck, not *Mister Who* or *Doctor X*, although all these titles may have rolled around in his mind. In the meeting, Martin says Sydney spoke of a little man inside a box who comes out, and when they asked him who he was he told them he was the Doctor, to which they asked Doctor Who? and he answered, 'Yes'.

As the months went by the series was developing under the watchful eyes of Verity's immediate boss Donald Wilson who reported back to Sydney. Electronics expert Mervyn Pinfield was also hugely significant, he was made associate producer due to his experience in that area, and he with Bernard Lodge, also devised the opening credits. Ron Grainer wrote the accompanying theme music which was arranged by Delia Derbyshire at the Radiophonic Workshop. To begin with Sydney and Donald were unsure about the opening titles, but Verity thought otherwise, and in the end they let her have her way. Experienced story-editor David Whitaker was brought in to help develop ideas, and it was at this point in time that Sydney remembers the idea of using a Police Box as the exterior to the ship first came about. The modern-day premise is that the Doctor knows his name but he doesn't utter it because of some dark and ancient occurrence, but this is not how the character was seen originally. The Doctor had no idea of who he was, and if Sydney had chosen to produce the show himself the memory loss would certainly have been more pivotal. Sydney's Doctor may have stumbled upon old foes he'd forgotten, but this doesn't happen in the early years of the show. It also seems unlikely the Doctor would never have heard of the Daleks when they first meet considering he is 740 years old.

Despite the assassination of John F. Kennedy affecting the viewing figures for the first episode of *An Unearthly Child*, the average for the other three episodes was 6.4 million which is in-line with the first two episodes of the following serial *The Daleks*. It was the third episode *The Escape* that saw a rapid jump in viewing figures with 8.9 million tuning in to watch on January 4 1964, and within a few weeks 'Dalekmania' was in full-swing, although it scared the kids out of their wits. The viewing figures alone would have been enough for Sydney already to see the show as a success, and he left it to the crew to get on with as he had other shows he needed to attend to.

At the BBC, every Wednesday morning there was a meeting called the Weekly Programme Review, where all the departmental heads got together to talk about the previous week's programmes and decided what was wrong and what was right about them. Some of the departmental heads voiced criticism that the Daleks were too frightening. I didn't agree with them, so I protested. The late Huw Wheldon, who as

Programme Controller was chairing the meeting, fortunately agreed with me. "Nonsense,' he roared out, 'I've got two little kids and they put waste paper baskets on their heads and run around yelling Exterminate! Exterminate!", and of course that calmed everything down. (Newman[6], 1986)

Doctor Who starting at 5:15 on a Saturday evening, and it soon grabbed the nation's hearts, despite letters from concerned parents saying the show was too creepy for their children. The formula of alternating an historical adventure with a futuristic one continued for quite some time, even though stories set in the past did worse in the ratings. An average of 9 million watched *The Daleks*, with the two-part *The Edge of Destruction* averaging a million more in February 1964. It was *The Aztecs* which first saw a consistent drop, but the historical stories continued to be made for quite some time because they showed children history, and besides the viewing figures for *The Aztecs* still averaged out at 7.5 million.

An idea which was suggested to Sydney by Kenneth Adam in 1964 was *The Wednesday Play* which would tap into a similar audience as *Armchair Theatre*, and was once again stoked the fires of 'kitchen sink' drama. Sydney coined the phrase 'agitational contemporaneity' to define these types of plays which were to be a series of social conflicts that challenged the norm, and some were a little too close to the bone for the BBC to risk airing. *The War Game* (1965) for example, tells the story of Britain after a nuclear attack by Russia, and such a threat was very real after the recent Cuban missile crisis, and it was banned at the time and didn't get shown until 1985. Sydney wanted to get away from the BBC's safe and unchallenging image, but sometimes they went too far.

Very much a vehicle for new talent such as the writer Dennis Potter, and actor-turned assistant story-editor Tony Garnett, *The Wednesday Play* was first aired in 1965, and it was groundbreaking in many ways. Garnett had met director Ken Loach the year before, and when they worked together on the series they produced gritty and engaging real-life drama's that grabbed everyone's attention. They brought to life Neil Dunn's *Up the Junction* in that first year which told the story of a young woman who got pregnant and had to seek out an illegal abortion. Ten million people watched it, although it was condemned by many, including Mary Whitehouse. Sydney never doubted the value of his work, it was his moral obligation to force these issues out into the open, and he wasn't finished with the sensors and critics yet. *Cathy Come Home* (1966) was another Garnett-Loach production which won the coveted Prix Italia award for drama, and told the story of a homeless single mother and her child. The play caused an uproar, and in the modern era it is viewed as one of the most a significant dramas ever produced. In 1998 *The Radio Times* readers voted it the best single drama of all time. Before any of this there was the problem of early Saturday evening programming to contend with, and to be successful he once again had to break with convention and he took a big risk on something that may have fallen flat on its face if the cynics had been listened to.

It is a person without imagination who cannot see that drama and interpretive documentary are the leading edge of social and human responsibilities. Cathy Come Home *did more to explain what is wrong with a bumbling, though well-meaning bureaucracy dealing with the homeless that all the statistics brought to us by politicians through the news media – a landmark production that! Alun Owen's poetic* 'The Rose Affair', *with its slick, beast-like multi-millionaire, told us something of the mysterious Paul Getty whom it is possible Alun at that time had not even heard of. (*Newman[7], 1976)

If *Armchair* was showing the here and now then *Doctor Who* gave viewers a vision of what the future might be like, and how it was in the past. The show challenged the way mankind lives on the Earth, and makes us think about how we may live out in space. Writers and producers who read Sydney's original memo and the BBC reports were privileged because of the creative freedom they were given, although they had to be aware of the limitations of budget, and what was acceptable for the new show. Having the whole of time and space was a massive canvass upon which they could paint their pictures.

Chapter Fifteen:
Back to Canada

During his time at the BBC Sydney was involved in some big shows that won many awards, none more so than the adaption of John Galsworthy's *The Forsyte Saga* novels which were one of the highlights of 1967. After giving up his position as Head of Serials to concentrate on the project, Donald Wilson wrote episodes that were rewarded with the BAFTA in 1968 for best serial. Eric Porter also won best actor for his portrayal of Soames Forsyte, and the department were responsible for yet another BAFTA thanks to Judi Dench's best actress performance in *Talking to a Stranger*. A further award went to John Hopkins for best writer, and Basil Coleman won best director for the opera *Billy Budd* which was remarkable because it would be vastly inferior listening on a TV set. The BBC could do culture as well as popular which proved that they hadn't lost touch with upper-classes. Sydney was presented with the Desmond Davis Award for Services to Television by BAFTA in 1968.

We've just done a terrific production of Benjamin Britten's Billy Budd... *The powers that be were persuaded by myself, that even though we were ignorant musically, we could get them to work with us, but the fact is opera singers have to act, and usually the most atrocious part of any opera is the acting.* (Newman[3], 1966)

Sydney had silenced those who may have doubted his abilities to transform ailing departments or shows during his time in Britain. What was even more significant was in doing this he helped gear-up the BBC drama department so that it was ready to face future competition. We must also consider how much of an influence the department had on so many millions of different people. From little children running around in the playground screaming "Exterminate", to religious groups debating the outrageous content of *Up the Junction*, recognising their mind-sets and prejudices helped many to change the way they thought about those that were different to them. Sydney set out to tell stories not to shock, but to show real life, warts and all. Despite the critics and the clashes he had with ITA and the National Viewers and Listeners Association he knew there had to be limitations and censorship. What made him revolutionary was not just his ability to know what audiences wanted and produce shows accordingly, he also knew how to walk the line and not let creativity get stifled by bureaucracy. Looking back at the effect he has had on society, and on the genre of science fiction there is evidence of a positive transformation. The messages *Armchair Theatre* and *The Wednesday Play* put out there challenged the establishment and thrust issues such as drug addiction and abortion out into the open, but Sydney's way of working wasn't for everybody.

Newman revamped the BBC's drama output, increasing the emphasis on serials and steering plays along more populist lines. His values were the polar opposite of (Don) Taylor's and the two were soon in conflict. Taylor particularly resented Newman's implementation of a "producer system", whereby directors were assigned scripts and had to work with separate script editors, rather than pursuing the work and writers they favoured, as Taylor was used to. Newman had divided out the roles of producer and director, which for plays had been combined under the producer title previously, leaving Taylor as director only for most of his productions. (Wake[2], 2010)

After some time of playing the Doctor William Hartnell's health had declined dramatically. He was suffering from arteriosclerosis and this made it difficult for him to concentrate and remember his lines. To the public he was *Doctor Who*, and the children and adults adored him in equal measure as the friendly uncle-type. He attended many functions and openings in character and always donated any fee to charity. By 1966, the show was a franchise making the BBC a considerable amount of money, and was one of the most watched shows in the country. Stories were also being sold abroad which proved to have been a good move which had lasting implications. Due to the BBC's policy of wiping episodes some of those that were sold to other countries became the only copy in existence. It was around this time that the *Doctor Who* producers started to believe the show was strong enough to continue without its leading star, after all Hartnell had not starred in the two *Doctor Who* movies that were made, and their thoughts would soon become reality.

Things went down-hill significantly for Hartnell after Verity Lambert left towards the end of 1965, and he did not get on with her successor John Wiles who he believed was taking the show in a different direction. Peter Cushing had played the Doctor in the two spin-off movies, *Dr. Who and The Daleks* (1965), and *Daleks – Invasion Earth: 2150AD* (1966) and they proved that *Doctor Who* could be popular with a different actor playing the Doctor. All that was needed was to think of a way of writing Hartnell out, and that is when they came up with the idea of regeneration, or as it was described at the time "renewal".

Innes Lloyd had the best relationship with Hartnell and took it upon himself to let him know of this decision. Lloyd sat Hartnell down and gently explained to him that he thought it was the best interest to the show, and to himself, if he "had a rest." Hartnell calmly agreed and a press release was put out to the papers that made it look like it was a mutual agreement between Hartnell and the BBC that he was to leave Doctor Who. *However, in reality, William Hartnell was deeply hurt and vindictively doubted that the show could last without him. As it is today, the public outcry to William Hartnell's departure was intense. Fans could not imagine* Doctor Who *without him. How was that going to work? The BBC itself was unsure about the future of* Doctor Who. *Nothing like this had ever been done before. Would the public accept a new actor as the Doctor?* (Tweedle, 2010)

Hartnell showed no animosity towards Patrick Troughton when he came in to shoot the regeneration sequence, but he said he had a nervous breakdown after he left the show. A few more roles on television and stage followed, the end of the 1960s saw him appearing in one show a year until 1970, when he played Henri Lindon in an episode of the courtroom drama *Crime of Passion*. He returned to the screen one last time for *The Three Doctors* in 1973, and by this time he was not well enough to travel to London so his parts were filmed at his home.

Afterwards his health deteriorated further and he died on April 23 1975.

The epic *The Daleks' Master Plan* ran for twelve weeks from November 1965, and the viewing figures for the whole series were just shy of nine-and-a-half million which meant it was a huge success. Sydney would have been aware of the situation with William Hartnell, but the veteran actor was old school and at best 'tolerant' of outsiders so any interjection by the head of the department would not have been welcomed. Sydney was also aware of the gaffs he was making as he occasionally tripped over his lines, and some of these were left in the final shows. There wasn't the time or the money to re-shoot, and it's fair to say the glory days were behind Hartnell and the ever-evolving team, although the popularity of the show, and the Daleks, was still at its height. Towards the end of his reign there was a downturn in viewing figures, the show had covered a lot of ground already, and was being surpassed by its American rival *Star Trek* which was filmed in glorious Technicolor, although it didn't arrive on British screens until the end of the decade. With the exception of *The Celestial Toymaker* none of Hartnell's last five stories hit the seven million viewers mark, and this included the regeneration story *The Tenth Planet*, which introduced the Cybermen.

It was only when Troughton took over that these figures were reached and surpassed. Already a seasoned actor, he was forty-six when he took on the role, and he didn't agree with what he was being asked to do by the production team, so Sydney stepped in and offered him some advice:

Patrick Troughton was unhappy being asked to produce a carbon copy of Hartnell's performance, so I suggested that he interpret the role like a 'cosmic hobo'. But still, the Doctor must never know how to operate the TARDIS. The earthlings should always want to get back home, and the Doctor should always intend to take them home, but they mistakenly end up somewhere in the past or in the future. (Newman[6], 1986)

There were always going to be critics, but most paid tribute to Sydney when he left, even some of the ones who had commented on him never reading Shakespeare. Not only had he been an outsider, he was also a heathen, The Bard just didn't interest him, it was too stuffy and restrictive, always there was a thirst for newness and originality and this was recognised by the Writers Guild of Great Britain who bestowed upon him the Zeta Award in 1970.

With his five-year contract due to run out in the summer of 1968, Sydney was feeling like he had done everything he could at the BBC. Splitting drama into three produced many successes. Andy Osborne's series department for example, had hits such as *Dr Finlay's Casebook, Softly Softly, Z Cars*, and *Adam Adamant Lives!*, which Sydney and Tony Williamson developed and Verity Lambert produced. Donald Wilson, and then Shaun Sutton headed up serials – alongside *Doctor Who* and *The Forsyte Saga* producing shows such as *Swizzlewick*, and *The Newcomers*. Single plays and operas were run by Gerald Savory, and *The Wednesday Play* had helped change the face of Britain despite those who opposed some of the themes that were explored. Besides it was pulling in up to twelve million viewers a week. The science-fiction series *Out of the Unknown*, which developed from *Out of this World*, was awarded first prize at the Fifth Festival Internazionale del Film di Fantascienza (International Science Fiction Film Festival) in Trieste on 17 July 1967, much to Sydney's delight.

Doctor Who was halfway through its fifth series with Patrick Troughton as the Doctor when Sydney left the BBC at the end of 1967. On October 12, 1967 *The Stage* reported that he had been offered a new contract, but had decided to turn it down. Change was needed, not just for Sydney but for *Doctor Who* too. The idea of regeneration was the key to the show's reinvention, and with new actors and directors it has been able to move with the times. It would however experience another downturn in viewing figures the following season, with episode eight of Troughton's final adventure *The War Games* doing particularly badly. After Sydney left he only followed the show from a distance, and the last story he oversaw was *The Enemy of the World*. A series of changes were on the horizon for the show at the end of the 1960s, including shooting it in colour, and a new Doctor, Jon Pertwee, ready to take an all-action approach.

Sydney had been offered the chance to be an executive producer for the Associated British Picture Company at Elstree Studios – the biggest rival to the Rank film empire. All the conditions were there for success, and he hoped he could cause a similar revolution in the British Film Industry to the one he'd created in television, although he knew only too well how difficult his job would be because of the vice-like grip of the American studios. In the preceding twelve years they had made films such as *The Dam Busters* (1955), and *Summer Holiday* (1963) and it was unfortunate that Sydney arrived a little too late as the industry was taking its last breath. By the end of the 1960s his creations *The Avengers*, *Doctor Who*, and *The Wednesday Play* were amongst the most popular shows on television, even though *Doctor Who* was the only one still being made after 1970. *Armchair Theatre* and *Out of the Unknown* were still enjoying success but he wasn't able to emulate any of this in British film which is something he always regretted. He spent 18 months there hearing promises and seeing no action at all.

In a year he developed four scripts, and on Christmas Eve 1968, he was given nearly a million dollars to make a film. The next day, the giant EMI recording and tape equipment firm bought ABPC and froze his funds. EMI decided not to make feature films and later, not to make films for TV. The story isn't widely known but there's no mystery about it. He didn't flop. (Vineberg, 1970)

Now fifty-years-old and frustrated as hell, Sydney thought completing the circle and moving back into film was the right thing to do at the start, and he was excited by the challenges ahead of him, but in truth the industry in Britain had been in decline for a number of years. With television and radio becoming ever more popular, British film-makers couldn't compete with the new technologies being employed by the big American studios. Sydney had been lucky enough to be at the right place, at the right time, with some great ideas when the medium of television was in its infancy, and he was able to have an effect. To do this again in the well-established film world would be a tall order, and just as it looked like things were about to happen his services were no longer required.

It was a bitter blow for a man who had been riding the crest of the wave just a short time before, although his hands were tied from the start. There were plans to make movies with a budget of a million pounds that could really put the studio back on the map that never got past the planning stage. All through his career he had been lucky, as well as skilful, but this time there was nothing he could do. As the 1960s drew to a close Sydney was beginning to feel like it was time to go home, and he had also been offered a job. The family had enjoyed their nine years in England, but things had changed politically in Canada. Sydney had done some amazing things, and he'd worked with some very talented people. These experiences stayed with him for the rest of his life and he returned to his adopted country whenever the occasion arose.

Chapter Sixteen
Homeward Bound

In early January 1970, Sydney and the family returned to Canada where he became the advisor to the chairman of the Canadian Radio and Television Commission who controlled broadcasting. He was appointed chairman of the National Film Board by the Prime Minister Pierre Trudeau eight months later and worked both jobs (Vineberg, 1970). At first he had said no to the NFB, but he changed his mind after talks with Secretary of State Gerard Pelletier. He'd just turned down the position of director of entertainment programming at CBC which he would have seen as a step backwards in his career. (Toronto Star, 1970) Film was where he wanted to be, and to get another chance after the disappointment of ABPC was great, although accepting both jobs could have taken him further away from the direct process of film making. 1965 had been his last production credit when he produced Harold Pinter's TV movie *The Tea Party.*, and his next was to be another 18 years.

With the children older and more independent, things were changing for the Newman family. Sydney was in his fifties when they returned to Canada, and with everything he had achieved perhaps he could have taken just one job, but instead he did the two, not because they needed the money, it was because he wanted to work, that was how it was. Rarely without a cigarette in his hand Sydney lived to for it, and that was exactly the sort of man Canadian film and TV needed. The CBC had suffered because they had lost a lot of their talent to the UK, and the film board had struggled for money after the government had frozen the budget. There was also indecisiveness in management which was hampering creativity. What was happening in Canada when Sydney returned was quite the reverse to how it had been before. All of the decent Canadian films were being made outside of the NFB, and Sydney was seen as the man to revive the organisation.

The board had been pregnant with trouble these last few years and there is wide recognition that a 'creative midwife' of proven talent has at last been found, an impresario that will bring forth something besides crises, and who is eager, as he put it last week, "to be boss for the first time in my life, make all the decisions and totally carry the can." (Vineberg, 1970)

At the Radio and Television Commission in Ottawa, Sydney's job was to make sure broadcasters lived up to their promises, and something he brought in was a guarantee that at least 60 percent of all content shown was Canadian. The trouble had started for the NFB in the mid-1950s, during and after the war they had a purpose, but they had run out of steam, and the freezing of the budget led to job losses. Film-makers marched on Parliament Hill, and the organisation's relationship with the CBC was at an all-time low, and none of the NFB's films had been shown at prime-time for many years. Sydney knew the board needed to be making films that people wanted to see, and the idea was to evolve groups of programs, and develop a close working relationship with the CBC. He believed if the board could prove the value of their work and become more commercial they would get more funding and get their films out to a greater audience.

One of the first things he did was look at theatrical distribution, and he found out the levels had been the same since 1952. He realised that short films weren't really shown in cinemas as they used to be, so he knew he would have to look at other methods. He had contacts at the CBC to help him get more material onto television, but the board also made a deal with CBS so some of their back-catalogue could be recorded onto video cassettes which could then be sold to schools, colleges, hospitals, and institutions. The system was called EVR, developed in the USA by Columbia, and the NFB were one of the first organisations to get in on the act.

The 1970s would see lots of changes in the way television was made and recorded, with colour TV becoming increasingly popular. It was David Attenborough, the BBC 2 controller, who was put in charge of the service, with the first colour broadcast, in the summer of 1967 of pictures being broadcast from Wimbledon. By 1968, most of the programmes on BBC 2 were made in colour, with BBC 1 following a few months later. By the end of the decade most of the programs on all three of the channels were in colour and, by the early 1970s, colour licence sales had gone up from 275,000 to 12 million. The *Doctor Who* story *Spearhead from Space* was not only the first story made in colour, it was also the only one to be shot entirely in film. The BBC cameramen were out on strike at the time, but the film cameramen were in a different union, so the whole story was shot in 16mm as Jon Pertwee's earthbound adventures began under the leadership of producer Barry Letts.

Canadians had been able to pick up colour transmissions from the USA since the mid-1950s, and the CBC's service started in 1966, with full colour arriving eight years later. At the board, Sydney reviewed the whole organisation from top to bottom, but when he joined he quickly put people's minds at rest and told them there would be no immediate changes. The organisation had been through so much turbulence that he knew he needed to promote stability. In November 1970, a meeting was arranged with John Grierson in attendance, alongside Andre Lamy who was Sydney's assistant, in which the future of the board was discussed. Sydney used some of his contacts at the BBC to put together another deal, and in December 1970 a collaboration was announced to produce three one-hour films for TV, with a budget set at $180,000. (Calgary Herald, 1970) After a few months Sydney had screened 240 of the board's films and come to the conclusion that many were too long, and their point could be put across in a lighter way. The screenings also helped him to find new talent, as well as weed out the people who were not moving in the same direction as him, and it wasn't long until the changes started to be felt.

Montreal – One year ago Canada's National Film Board was at perhaps the lowest ebb of its 31-year history. The creative staff, its confidence eroded, felt its future and its art threatened by a government-imposed austerity budget. Morale took a nose-dive and the cohesiveness which characterised earlier board efforts was on the verge of crumbling. Today however, there is a renewed spirit in the board's Montreal office, largely due to new leaders whose presences seems to have the exhilarating effect of a sea-salt breeze. (Pascoe, 1971)

A deal was eventually struck between the CBC and the film-board but it caused uproar because adverts were shown at intervals during the film. Sydney didn't see it as a problem, but there were some at the board who still believed the purity of art outweighing commercial demands and, whilst he understood their philosophy he had to see the whole process as a system, and he needed to walk the line. He wanted their films to be seen by as many people as possible, but there were people who would have preferred to have not shown them rather than have ad breaks. This was a noble approach but it was the sponsors who were paying the artists' wages.

Sydney had the NFB cameras in place for a nautical protest in 1971. 11 peace protestors went to the Aleutian Island of Amchitka to try and stop nuclear tests that were being conducted by the USA. The mission was paid for by a concert in Vancouver by Joni Mitchell, James Taylor and Phil Ochs. The ship in which they sailed was renamed *Greenpeace*, leading to the beginning of the non-violent activist organisation. Trouble brewed when they asked the NFB if they could have the footage back, in the end the ship had to turn around because the firing date was changed, and they weren't happy with the length of time it took the NFB to give the film back via a telegram as the protestors believed that there was a political reason for not handing the footage back straight away. Sydney said that he wasn't even aware of their message as he was away at the time, and that their allegations were totally unfounded, with the film not being finished because they didn't shoot enough footage. He wasn't pleased when they threatened legal action, and he told them they would develop the film and present it to the organisation when it was ready. (Vineberg, 1972)

By the summer of 1971, things had turned around at the NFB, and Sydney told the Press that more of their films had been seen in theatres in the past year than ever before. There was more trouble around the corner however, and Sydney had to step in and cancel work on a film in 1972 which showed the Canadian political and economic system being overthrown. He believed it was not in the best interests of the country, and that the vast majority of Canadians who believed in democracy would never forgive him if it was ever released. Titled *Vingt-quatre Heures ou Plus* by Gilles Grouix, Sydney watched the cutting-room copy and was appalled, serving to highlight the fundamental difference in the types of films and programs he was involved in. (The Montreal Star, 1972) To make a straightforward hard-hitting film of such significance really was a challenge to the establishment – after all funds were coming from the people, and the movies they made were for the people.

To directly advocate revolution went too far, and under his guidance Sydney had shown people far subtler ways to make waves with film, it was the whole point of the 'kitchen sink'. Even more subtle was the way science fiction went about this, a controversial topic could be set in the far reaches of space using aliens, and this would take the sting out of it. For example the *Doctor Who* adventure *Colony in Space*, which aired the year before, told the story of a group of struggling colonists in a far off world, and how they battled against 'The Corporation' and their ruthless leader Captain Dent, who is killing them. If such an adventure was set on Earth, in a particular country, using a familiar company name, there would have been hell to pay.

In 1973 *Doctor Who* was celebrating its tenth anniversary – Sydney was amazed, and continued to feel that away. Many of the people who worked with him over the years have commented on his directness, but he had a way of doing it that at least minimised any offence. There were others such as Ted Kotcheff who just took it on the chin and realised that he was usually right, and he had to get that information into their heads. People shouldn't stop living when they got behind a camera or were directing a TV show, he wanted them to come alive. If the director and the producer didn't believe it, then how would the viewers at home? Over the years Sydney criticised *Doctor Who* on more than one occasion – he even spoke poorly of it because of some of the directions it took during its original run – although he was always proud of it as a concept, and for the fame it had, but no so much for the fortune others made from it.

There were many storms to ride when he returned to Canada, but once again the changes being made had helped the board turn the corner. There was a considerable backlash over the banning of Grouix's film, and Sydney was called a 'Little Latin American Dictator' and other unpleasant things by Ottawa's leading film-makers. In February 1972, John Grierson died, bringing to an end an era in film-making. The following year the founder of documentary, and the biggest influence on Sydney's life as a young film-maker, was honoured with his own one-hour CBC special.

Another honour came Sydney's way two days before *Doctor Who*'s tenth anniversary in November 1973. At the annual Canadian Motion Picture Pioneers dinner in Toronto he was presented with a special award for his contribution to the development of the Canadian film industry by the President Leonard Bernstein and he was delighted. It was not the only award he had received, alongside the Zeta he was given The Desmond Davis Award in 1967, and was made a Knight of Mark Twain by the 'International Mark Twain Society', and a life-member of the Directors Guild of Canada. (Bush, 1973) He must have been doing something right, although running the NFB was not an easy job. Even in John Grierson's time half the battle had been dealing with bureaucracy and over the years Sydney's method of keeping as much of that at arm's length as possible was extremely useful. For him it was all about making good films that could be seen by as many people as possible. The NFB's annual report for 1973/74 was welcome news as it showed an approximate 794 million had viewed their films during that period. (Lysyshyn, 1974)

In August 1974, having organised the board's 35th birthday celebrations successfully, Sydney approached the last twelve months of his contract and, although he had achieved a lot he still felt there was more to do. He hoped to continue, but was instead moved to an advisory position in Ottawa. He was proud of his time in charge, even though at times it had been a white-knuckle ride. One of the problems that he had in Canada was not being bilingual, and he was accused on more than one occasion of not understanding French-Canadians. He was also 58 years old, so time was against him. Not so much a relic of the past – his expert advice was sought by many – but a younger generation were now making films.

Chapter Seventeen
Becoming a Legend

On April 2, 1974 Jon Pertwee got up off the floor and was replaced by Tom Baker in the final scenes of Barry Letts's story *Planet of the Spiders*, and introduced the world to another new Doctor, and a virtual unknown who was going to play the fourth reincarnation. Tom was born in Liverpool in January 1934 to a devout Catholic mother, and a father who was in the Merchant Navy, he struggled academically and failed the eleven plus. When he was fifteen he decided to become a monk, much to his mother's delight, but as the years passed he became more disillusioned with monastic life. At 21, he decided to leave, and after National Service he went to drama school and joined the National Theatre in 1968. A bit-part actor during the 1960s and 1970s, sometimes money was tight and he would seek other work, and around this time he worked on a building site and operated a Kangol drill. Desperate for acting work he wrote to Bill Slater who he knew, and he was just about to become the Head of Serials at the BBC. After watching Tom in *The Golden Voyage of Sinbad* Bill soon realised he had found the next *Doctor Who*.

After the death of his friend Roger Delgado, and with Letts and Terrance Dicks also leaving, it felt like the end of an era for Jon Pertwee, and he decided it was time to go. He let the head of programming Sean Sutton know he would stay for one more season if he could get a pay-rise, and Sutton told him they'd be sorry to see him go. When Baker took to the air for his first full story *Robot* on 28 December 1974, Sydney was into his last year at the NFB, and he held lots of other jobs and titles at this time including: Trustee at the Nation Arts Centre in Ottawa, board member and film development director at the CBC, and in 1975 he became special advisor on film to the Canadian Secretary of State. He would later admit he had been plagued by the political landscape in Canada during his second spell at the board, and had become entangled in a number of events. The government was not as committed financially to filmmaking and the arts at this point in time, and this always frustrated Sydney because he felt he could have done more.

I saw it happening in Canada back in the 1960s. Governments simply don't like commotion about themselves. They are killing their own child in Canada and it's happening with the BBC as well. Why many of us leave Canada is that Canada cannot afford group art anymore. (Newman[11], 1987)

On another occasion Sydney called his time at the board a disaster, but there were still many fine moments, and there was always something going on. 1973 saw some very special visitors to the area, the first was Indian Prime Minister Indira Gandhi in June. She came to promote unity and trade between the two countries, but this would all fall apart. In May the following year India violated an agreement by testing a nuclear bomb produced by a Canadian reactor, and the Canadian government was up in arms. Despite this, Sydney never lost the deep respect he had for the lady, and in January 1974 he sent her a letter, and a copy of the short film they made about of her visit, and thanked his staff for making it happen.

I would like personally to express my appreciation to all members of staff for the part they play in making Madame Indira Gandhi's visit to the National Film Board on June 21st such a charming and worthwhile occasion.

The very tight schedule and the tight security arrangements did not allow Madame Gandhi the opportunity to see more of the Board's work, people and installations. In addition, the Prime Minister expressed the wish to use the limited time at her disposal to meet some of our film-makers rather than officials and those in other staff functions.

Many have told me that Madame Gandhi considered her time at the board to be the highlight of her Canadian visit thus far. Congratulations and thanks to you all for helping to make it that in every way – including the cheerful farewell as the Prime Minister departed. (Newman[10], 1973)

Queen Elizabeth II toured Alberta and Saskatchewan in July 1973, to celebrate the centennial of the Royal Canadian Mounted Police. She would be back again in 1976, to open the Olympics in Montreal. In Saskatchewan, Her Majesty dedicated Queen Elizabeth Court, in front of Regina's city hall. In Ottawa, in August 1973, the governor general Roland Michener presented her with a film called *Centaur* on behalf of Sydney and the NFB. Looking back on his time, Sydney recognised that he gave the NFB the shot in the arm it needed, but at the end things were too 'cliquey', and treading softly was not his greatest talent. Throughout his career he told it like it was, but it was constructive criticism, although it could get heated. There was no time to think about people's feelings if there was money and his reputation at stake, but nobody could have ever called him a bully or disrespectful. His last day at the NFB was August 21, 1975 and he made it clear that he still felt part of the board, even though he was no longer in charge.

It wasn't that Sydney hated what *Doctor Who* had become towards the end of the 1970s and into the 1980s, it was more of a dislike, and he did see the beginning of its demise in the 1980s. Tom Baker's Doctor gave the show a much needed boost because of course he was the Doctor who first became popular in America. Sydney watched from a distance and he felt it had lost its way as it moved on from its 20th anniversary in November 1983. Because of constraints such as budget, and the fact that so much of it was shot in the studio, the show sometimes lacked realism, and some of the latex monsters the Doctor encountered were the stuff of his worst nightmares, bloody BEMs!

Sydney continued to work as a creative consultant, and as a producer in the latter part of his career, and was awarded with the Order of Canada in medal in 1981 which is the second highest honour in the country. There were many trips back to England, especially after his beloved wife Betty died on December 5 that year. She had been ill for quite some time and suffered from multiple sclerosis (Knelman, 1997) but her passing was a shock to Sydney and their three daughters, and he never fully recovered. He was not good on his own; she had been the person who kept everything spinning so he could create his films. She had dealt with the sleepless nights and the dirty nappies, and had stood with him on every big decision he made. She was a wife and a mother, but she'd also written material when it was needed, and was a technical-coordinator and chief negative-cutter who also had theatre plays produced in Canada and the USA. (Montreal Gazzette, 1981) Sydney would find companionship once again towards the end of his life with a new partner Marion McDougall.

As the 1980s wore on *Doctor Who* fell out of favour with the BBC hierarchy, but they couldn't scrap it. There'd be too much of a backlash, and besides the ratings were still good. Tom Baker's final story *Logopolis* started on Saturday February 28 1981, and it averaged out at almost 6.7 million viewers. When the series returned with new Doctor Peter Davison in 1982, they showed his opening four-parter *Castrovalva* on successive Monday and Tuesday nights, and it averaged 9.6 million. The ratings were up for the year, but for the 20th anniversary season they switched once again to successive Tuesday and Wednesday nights, with the one off special *The Five Doctors* airing on Wednesday 23 November 1983. Davison's final season was shunted further along to Thursday and Fridays, but there was still no real concern because audiences never dipped lower than six million. Even when the sixth Doctor Colin Baker took over in *The Twin Dilemma* at the end of season twenty-one, and with the story judged one of *Doctor Who*'s lowest points, people were still tuning in. By now the show was becoming a hot potato, and nobody knew what to do with it. For season twenty-two they switched it back to Saturday nights, but the ratings collapsed the following year (1986) for *The Trial of a Time Lord* season which made BBC Controller Michael Grade pick up the telephone in desperation and call the show's creator.

In the mid-1980's, Doctor Who *was in a bit of a slump. The rating weren't what they once were, viewers weren't connecting with Colin Baker's abrasive Sixth Doctor, and BBC executives were keen to cancel the show altogether (which they finally did in 1989).*

Doctor Who *creator Sydney Newman agreed that something had to change, calling Colin Baker's second season "largely socially valueless, escapist schlock" in a 1986 letter to BBC One controller Michael Grade with his thoughts on how to restore* Doctor Who *to its former glory.* (Rice, 2016)

The most revolutionary thing Sydney told Grade was that he believed the show could be revived by turning the Doctor into a heroine, and it would have certainly fit in with more recent developments in Time Lord physiology in which arch enemy the Master turned into a female in the new series, and for each recent new regeneration the press had said a female has been in the picture. In 1986, the BBC decided to play it safe, although names such as Joanna Lumley and Dawn French were suggested at the time.

In a written pitch dated October 6, 1986, the Canadian-born television executive delivered a scathing verdict on the show's populist, dumbed-down drift and called on Mr Grade to "engage the concerns, fears and curiosity" of young viewers. He implored: "Don't you agree that this is considerably more worthy of the BBC than Doctor Who*'s presently largely socially valueless, escapist schlock!"*

Mr Newman urged the controller to temporarily reintroduce Patrick Troughton, a former Time Lord, to steady the TARDIS and pave the way for the most radical change in the show's 23-year history. He wrote: "At a later stage Doctor Who should be metamorphosed into a woman. This requires some considerable thought – mainly because I want to avoid a flashy, Hollywood Wonder Women *because this kind of heroine with no flaws is a bore. Given more time than I have now, I can create such a character."* (Horne, 2010)

For a while it seemed as a reprise may be on the cards for Sydney, and he also told Grade that he would be willing to become Executive Producer of the show, and he also requested that his name be added to the closing credits. There were one or two other projects on the boil at the time, one being a drama about 'The Bloomsbury Group' for Channel Four, and he once again threw himself into his work, but this time without Betty to go home to, and with his age against him, getting a project off the ground proved to be a step to far. The ideas he had given Grade were perhaps a little too off-the-wall, like the inclusion of a trumpet-playing girl wearing John Lennon glasses and her graffiti-spraying brother.

He also requested his name be added to the programme's closing titles. However, Grade spurned the advice of the veteran, who died in 1997, and choose instead to replace Colin Baker with Sylvester McCoy. The move failed to reverse the show's diminishing ratings and the original series was quietly axed.

In 1983 Sydney's was associate producer of a Canadian comedy movie called *Utilities*. Released in June it was reported to have had a budget of six million dollars and starred Robert Hays and Brooke Adam. Towards the end of 1980s people turned to him for his advice on scripts and other production matters, and his opinion was especially valued after the cancelation of *Doctor Who* in 1989. On February 15, 1987, just seven weeks short of his 70th birthday, he was honoured with a 40 minute prime-time documentary on Channel Four which made the headlines, but after failing in any further bids to make a television show he returned to Canada and settle in Governors Bridge. Sydney's last production credit was as producer for the Christmas 1989 broadcast of Benjamin Britten's opera *The Little Sweep* for Channel 4. He was never involved with *Doctor Who* fandom, but he did interviews for television and magazines whenever he was asked to and in later years he painted and created works of art on his computer. (Spears, 1997) To celebrate the NFBs 50th anniversary in 1989, another documentary was made in Canada and many of the former members of staff were interviewed, including Sydney, and they shared their memories of those distant days now long-gone. Distant days when legends were being made, and in his last years Sydney would sit quietly in his chair and contemplate it all with a smile. In the latter years of his life Sydney's health declined rapidly and he suffered from emphysema. He passed away on Thursday 30 October 1997 in Toronto after suffering two heart-attacks. He was 80 years old. The shows he created will live on in the hearts and minds of people for many generations to come, and *Doctor Who* (which many doubted would last beyond 13 weeks) may well prove as durable as the works of Shakespeare in thousands of years to come. There could be no more fitting a tribute to the man who thought outside the box.

REFERENCES

Bareham, P. (2013) *Armchair Theatre: The Greatest Man in the World* http://islandofterror.blogspot.co.uk/2013/05/armchair-theatre-greatest-man-in-world.html (Accessed 3.2.17)

Bunch, A (2013) *The Torontonian roots of Doctor Who — the Canadian behind the legendary TV show.*

Bush, G. (1973) *NFB News Release: Picture Pioneers honor NFB's Newman. November 21.* http://spacing.ca/toronto/2013/11/26/torontonian-roots-doctor-canadian-behind-legendary-tv-show/ (Accessed 12.12.15)

Calgary Herald (1970) *Canada and Britain join in triple-film production. Dec 5.*

CBC Digital Archives http://www.cbc.ca/archives/entry/1952-cbc-television-debuts (Accessed 3.1.17)

CBC Press Service (1957) *First Performance.* Toronto, Canada.

Cox, K. (1979) *The Grierson Files. Cinema Canada,* Montreal.

Fiddy, D. (2016) *Leonard White: Television producer who helped create 'The Avengers', in charge as it developed from gritty drama to witty escapism.* The Independent, Jan 2016.

Falk, Q (1974) *Canada's Film Board Teach the world – Sydney Newman.* Daily Cinema, March 23, 1974. London.

Flint, D (2013) *Pathfinders in Space finally comes to DVD* https://wipednews.com/tag/early-sci-fi-tv-shows/ (Accessed 28.2.17)

Graham, R. (2016) http://abcatlarge.co.uk/sydney-newman/ (Accessed 12.8.16)

Greatorex, W. (1961) *The Canadian Who Changed British TV.* The Star Weekly Magazine, March 11.
Hilmes, M. (2010) *The North Atlantic triangle: Britain, the USA, and Canada in 1950s television.* Media History Journal. Volume 16, Issue 1.

Horne, M. (2010) *How Doctor Who Nearly Became the Time Lady.* The Telegraph, October 10.

Howe, D. Walker, S. (1994) *Doctor Who: The Handbook: The First Doctor.* Virgin Publishing, ISBN 0 426 20430 1.

Keel, J. (2002) The Avengers Forever; Behind the Scenes http://www.theavengers.tv/forever/keel-prod-dp3.htm (Accessed 28.2.17)

Knelman, M (1997). *Lives Lived – Sydney Newman.* The Globe and Mail, 25 November.

Knowles,V. (2007) *Strangers at Our Gates: Canadian Immigration and Immigration Policy, 1540-2006: Canadian Immigration and Immigration Policy, 1540-2007.* Dundurn, Toronto.

Laurence M, Hulse B.
http://www.televisionheaven.co.uk/sydney_newman.htm {Accessed 12.12.16)
Lysyshyn, J. (1974) *NFB News Release: NFB Annual Report Shows Active Year.* December 18.

McWilliams, D. (1990) *Creative Process: Norman McLaren.*

Newman, G. (2015) Notes: Sydney's daughter Gillie in conversation with Ryan Danes.

Newman[1] S. (1975) *Statement of the Government Film Commissioner, Sydney Newman, to the Standing Committee on broadcasting, films, and assistance arts, p6.* (15.4.75)

Newman[2], S. (2006) *Doctor Who Origins.* (Video)

Newman[3], S. (1966) *Doctor Who creator Sydney Newman discusses his career with CBC.* (Video)
https://www.youtube.com/watch?v=LUilWt_mFZA

Newman[4], S. Webber, C. (1963) *'Dr. Who': General notes on Background and Approach.* BBC Archives.

Newman[5], S. (1959) *The Armchair Theatre Publication.*

Newman[6], S. (1986) Sydney Newman.
https://drwhointerviews.wordpress.com/tag/sydney-newman/(Accessed 12.2.16)

Newman[7], S. (1976) *Notes for the James McTaggart Memorial Lecture.* London, September 20.

Newman[8], S. (1971) *The Secret NFB. An address by Sydney Newman.* November 25.

Newman[9], S. (1972) *Address by Sydney Newman Canadian Government Film commissioner and chairman National Film Board of Canada to the Soviet Association of film-makers.* June 1972.

Newman[10], S. (1973) *NFB Memo: To All Members of Staff.* June 27.

Newman[11], S. (1987) *UK Honours Canadian Who Put Everyman On Screen.* The Edmonton Journal, February 10.

Newman[12], S. (1976) *Notes for Centennial lecture series.* November 18.

Ohayon, A. (2014) *'Canada Carries On' and the postwar years: The National Film Board in transition.*
http://blog.nfb.ca/blog/2014/05/14/canada-carries-on-postwar-years/(Accessed 12.1.17)

Pascoe, C. (1971) *Newman-Lamy team revive NFB.* Ottawa Journal, March 3.

Pratley, G (1982). *The Toronto Sun* (15.1.82)

Rice, B (2015) *Doctor Who Creator Sydney Newman Wanted a Female Doctor.* https://doctorwhowatch.com/2015/06/15/doctor-who-creator-sydney-newman-wanted-a-female-doctor/. (Accessed 1.3.17)

Sellers, R (2012) *Don't let the Bastards Grind You Down: How One Generation of British Actors changed the World,* Arrow Publishing.

Spears, T (1997) *Obituary Sydney Newman: Producer Created Avengers.* Ottawa Citizen, November 1.

Strange, C (1977) *CBC Television Special,* October 23rd. (Video) http://www.cbc.ca/archives/entry/1952-cbc-television-debuts (Accessed 9.2.17)

Sullivan, S (2016) http://www.shannonsullivan.com/drwho/serials/a.html (Accessed 2.2.17)

Tessler, D (2014) http://www.televisionheaven.co.uk/pathfinders_in_space.htm (Accessed 2.2.17)

The Montreal Star (1972) *NFB cancels Film Urging Revolution.* December 12.

The Montreal Gazette (1981) *TV writer Betty McRae.* December 8.

Toronto Telegraph (1971) *NFB Chiefs Eulogy.* March,27.

Toronto Star (1970) *Sydney Newman Appointed Head of National Film Board.*

Tweedle, S. (2010) *Regenerations: The Madness of William Hartnell.* http://popcultureaddict.com/television/williamhartnellii/ (Accessed 1.2.17)

Vahimagi, T. (2014) http://www.screenonline.org.uk/people/id/522017/index.html (Accessed 3.1.17)

Vineberg, D. (1970) *I don't know what I'm going to be fighting for.* The Montreal Star, August 22.

Vineberg, D. (1972) *Amchitka charge denied by NFB commissioner.* The Montreal Star, April 6.

Wake, O. (2013) *Underground* (1958). http://www.britishtelevisiondrama.org.uk/?p=4313 (Accessed 19.1.17)
Wake[2], O. (2010) *Don Taylor* http://www.britishtelevisiondrama.org.uk/?tag=don-taylor (Accessed 21.2.17) http://www.britishtelevisiondrama.org.uk/?p=4313(Accessed 5.9.15)

Williams-Rautiolla, S (2005) http://www.museum.tv/eotv/captainvideo.htm (Accessed 12.5.16)

Afterword

Ryan Danes

Doctor Who is now in its 54th year, and has changed its shape and form so many times over the decades. Like the time-space machine TARDIS itself it has ebbed and flowed through the years, some of the changes have brought about great success, others have set it on a path of disaster, uproar and cancellation. It could be argued that today's show would be unrecognisable to Sydney Newman; a one-time low-budget BBC science-fiction show is now a worldwide franchise which can rival any in the world of TV and film.

Since the publishing of the first edition of this book the role of Australian writer Antony Coburn, and the amount of work he did towards the formulation of the show, has come to light. Only some of this made it through to the broadcasted show, and I felt it necessary to include a biography from his son, Stef Coburn, which has been specially written for this second edition of this book, as well as reprinting the original un-edited version of his father's short story as an added bonus.

As the show moves forwards into new realms I feel it is an appropriate time to look back at where its origins, and at the impact two 'colonials' who had spent between them just over fifteen years of their lives in England when the first episode of the iconic British show was aired.

THE TALE OF THE FOURTH STRANGER

by
Anthony Coburn

Copyright © 2017 Estate of Anthony Coburn

All rights reserved

O.C.R. and retyping by Dallas Jones

Introduction
By Stef Coburn

It may seem odd to some, that for the purposes of a book about Sydney Newman, the nominal 'creator', though, in reality perhaps more accurately the 'instigator', of *Doctor Who*; I've been asked to introduce a non *Doctor Who* related short story, written by my late father, James Anthony Coburn.

Before anyone questions such an inclusion, in a book about Sydney, which, of course, very likely only exists at all as a result of his seminal involvement in *Doctor Who*, the following facts should be understood.

It is a fact that, in instigating his intended, revolutionary new BBC children's science fiction show, in April of 1963, Sydney Newman, in essence, asked his various underlings of the time, for a story about 'a crotchety old man with a space and time machine'; and that beyond subsequent executive decisions approving or disapproving the suggestions of the various others, he at this stage or that, assigned to the task thereafter, Sydney made no further personal contributions to the creative content of the show.

It is similarly a fact, that the writer, who by virtue of a combination of circumstance and personal ability, found himself saddled with the task of 'fleshing-out' sculpting and giving animated colourful expression to Sydney's barest of bare-bones outlines, was my father, James Anthony Coburn, who preferring his middle name to the forename he shared with his own father, signed himself Anthony throughout his adult life; habitually shortened amongst his friends and adult familiars (amongst whom I now retro-actively count myself), to plain 'Tony'.

As has been previously published elsewhere, it is my personal recollection of the afternoon of Saturday 10th of August, three days after my ninth birthday, which is my strongest and most oft repeated *Doctor Who* related memory of the period. When my father, called for supper, from his study – from which the sounds of furious bursts of typing, punctuated by the violently abrupt 'brrrrrpp – TING!' of his typewriter's carriage-return had been heard repeatedly throughout the day – came practically running down the stairs, to the kitchen / breakfast room in which myself and a younger brother, sat waiting for our mother, to put out whatever now long forgotten meal it was she had prepared, bursting excitedly into the room with the words: "Get a load of this, boys! 'TARDIS', 'Time And Relative Dimension In Space'!" His new creation, leaving his lips for the first time ever in company, since metaphorically 'materialising' earlier that same afternoon, in his mind.

With Tony's independent addition of the proper name for *Doctor Who*'s most enduring fifth (at the time) basic character: the sentient sapient time and space travelling entity named 'Time And Relative Dimension In Space', shortened, for utility and convenience, to the now World Famous acronym, 'TARDIS'; coming on top of his suggestion three months earlier of the 'police box' exterior for the Doctor's means of transportation and his less visible but every bit as enduring derivation from his own personality, of the essential traits attitudes and mannerisms of *Doctor Who*'s otherwise periodically mutating eponymous central character, it is hard to dispute, that in doing so he became, to all intents and purposes, not merely *Doctor Who*'s first transmitted scriptwriter, but its essential 'co-creator', without whose core contributions, whatever product, assuming any, might in such an eventuality, have made it to the screen, would of a certainty, have born little if any resemblance to the show that actually did; which, of course, this book about Sydney exists in context of.

With Tony's pivotal involvement in Sydney's signature project thus established, my principal purpose here, is by no means, to add yet more 'blather' to the largely speculative and often erroneous reams already variously produced by this person or that on the subject of my father's involvement in *Doctor Who*, but instead to introduce an earlier (likely significantly so, but more about that later) work of his; published here for the purposes of acquainting the interested reader with Tony's precursor and later works: to whit: his long out of print, short story, *The Tale of the Fourth Stranger*.

The tale of 'The Tale'

First published in April of 1959, in *The Saturday Evening Post* and subsequently, in quick succession, in June of the same year, in the *Suspense* monthly story anthology, the story's date of actual composition is unclear. In attempting to derive a probable date, from appraisal of its circumstances, content and style, two different possibilities suggest themselves.

The most obvious wild guess, would be to place it at some point in the years or months immediately preceding its first publication in *The Saturday Evening Post*; written perhaps for a spot of light relief, after or away from, his other substantially greater literary exertions of the period. Perhaps also as a salve for his recurring profound sense of homesickness for his faraway native land. There are however, significant difficulties with this.

In the period between the completion of his play, *The Bastard Country* in 1957, and its subsequent publication, and first performance, in Sydney, in 1959 (then Birmingham, UK, in 1960), Tony was, pre-occupied in the main (in addition to the mundane practical considerations increasingly laid upon him by his by then annually / bi-annually expanding family) with his frustrating protracted, and ultimately unsuccessful attempts to see his dramatic masterpiece launched on the World stage.

If placing *The Tale of the Fourth Stranger* after the completion of *The Bastard Country* in '57' is therefore problematic, for broadly similar reasons, placing it at any earlier point in the activity packed years since his arrival in the UK, seems even more so.

In the seven years, since disembarking at Southampton, Tony had made his way to London; found 'digs'; introduced himself to, joined, and become a quickly 'rising star' in, a Catholic discussion group; met a girl; gone proselytising; married the girl; and set about attempting to breed his own aspirationally communion-taking cricket team, whilst simultaneously conceiving, gestating, and writing the work he hoped and dared imagine would take him to the West End, Broadway and beyond.
Beyond Broadway, in 1959?

Where, you may well ask, might that be?

Born in December of 1927, growing up in a suburb of Melbourne, Tony wrote short stories and plays throughout his childhood. As a teenager he worked as a 'cub' reporter for the *Melbourne Argus*, just long enough to comprehend that his literary ambitions were for the foreseeable future likely to remain unfulfilled in the culturally primitive Australia of the time; the gathering realisation that this was so, driving him to precipitously depart his childhood home and his native soil, at the age of 20. Barely into manhood, and full of dreams of 'making it' as a dramatist on the World stage, he booked passage in 1950, aboard the passenger steamer, SS Mooltan, sailing, recklessly far, at so tender an age, from the bosom of his extended family.

Well understanding, as he must have at the time, that he would in all probability be away for years, it likely nevertheless did not for one moment occur to him, that he would never see his father again; that he would contrive to spend just a single summer season more in his mother's company, during her sole visit, in advancing years, to the UK; or, worst of all, that he would not set foot again in the longed for country of his birth for in excess of two decades; and then only for an activity packed working visit, lasting a fleeting six months, before the remorseless necessities of his life pulled him away once more, back to his home and career in the south of England; never again to return.

Simply put, my father's most treasured personal goal, from as far back as I personally can remember, and throughout the twenty three years, I knew him, remained his fondly articulated 'dream' of returning 'home', to the doubtless enthusiastic welcome of his celebrating compatriots, in vindicating triumph, aboard the yacht he dreamed of buying, but never could afford; Skippered and navigated by himself, crewed of course, by his bemused if doubtless by then ocean-seasoned, long past seasick brood; fed and quite possibly figureheaded by his doted upon, first and only mate.

Stranded, as he found himself, half a planet away from his parents, his two younger brothers, and the culture that had raised him, it's certainly possible that composing *The Tale of the Fourth Stranger*, steeped, as it is in its semi-mythical, uniquely Australian setting, may have been a means to afford himself some brief moments of mental re-immersion at least in the atmosphere of his far off native land.

It is the noticeably florid prose style of *The Tale of the Fourth Stranger* however, which hints at a more likely explanation, by far. That the story was in fact composed many years earlier; by a much younger 'Tony', set down, quite possibly long before thoughts of moving to a far off foreign country even occurred, at some or other time in his now largely obscure early years, the details of which, whether lost to the attrition of intervening decades, or simply going unrecorded at the time, will likely now remain forever mysterious.

Contrasted with the greatly more economical use of language in Tony's later 'works' the difference in style is marked. Suggesting not so much the experimental feeler into a consciously lyrical epic dramatic prose, which a later composition date might have suggested, so much as an aspirationally over-achieving much younger writer, straining to showcase his self-suspected nascent genius in every line; enthusiastically loosing every metaphorical arrow in his literary quiver, so as to speak, in a relentless hail of multisyllabic descriptive adjectives, leaving none in any doubt as to his command of the language; whilst unsuspectingly all the while running the risk of overwhelming his reader's attention to his narrative thread, with his constant barrage of linguistic fireworks.

Of the two possibilities: written earlier or written later, in the likely permanent absence of a definitive answer, I'm going for the former, mostly for the reasons stated above, but also for the impression I'm left with having just read it again, for only the second time in my life, of the uncomplicated purity of its character. Whatever the story, behind the story, the tale itself remains quintessentially Australian in the otherworldly atmosphere it evokes, putting me in mind of Australian director Peter Weir's iconic *Picnic at Hanging Rock*, with its apparent unconnectedness to anywhere or anything falling outside its own dreamlike context.

It's not that Tony couldn't have written it, sitting in flickering electric light under grey London skies. Only that, forced for better or worse to make his bed henceforth amongst the infinitely more prosaic 'bloody Poms'; with the cyan skies, the bright crystal seas, and the great baked brown expanses of his far off beloved country, to all intents and purposes lost to him; compelled to look forward instead, to deal as best he could with whatever came next, I do not, on reflection, think that he would.

– o O o –

So here is the original un-edited version of the short story re-typed directly from Anthony Coburn's carbon copy.

THE TALE OF THE FOURTH STRANGER

Part 1

I always believe legends. However fantastic they may sound to others and even sometimes to me, I believe them; and they have made my life richer and more varied than any I know. Mad people everywhere, of course, think I am mad, and this amuses me; for where I take all mythical bulls by the horns and wrestle with them in a great adventure, they purse their lips and smile knowingly and pass on unchanged, except for the worse, for ever having listened at all. A sad world this, where a man may travel from his own country and find all men everywhere as quaint, impracticable, unworldly, and all their stories and folklore as subtle traps for his credulity. So to The Devil with a cynical generation and may it burn on a fire of fairy tales: for my part I can travel the globe in ease and plenty because in my youth I was strong as an ox, I was fleet as a deer, I had the courage of a lion, I could swim like the great tiger shark himself, and I believed everything I was told.

It happened long ago when my hair was fair and plentiful and my muscles readily tingled to the warm sun, that I lay on a soft sandy beach and dreamed out at the sea. Before me stretched the watery mass of Port Phillip Bay, and it gurgled and hissed for my delight on a hot December afternoon. This Bay cradles the great City of Melbourne but I was far from there in mind as well as body, for whenever the sun returned to the south my grip loosened at its spinning centre and I was thrown from it; through the air like a sea bird to its home. People has long ceased saying that I would never amount to anything, for in that year it was no more a mark of wisdom than saying a rainy day was wet. I was a slave to sun and the water's edge when my youth was at the full in Oomallunga Inlet.

This small fishing village had caught me in flight and drawn me to earth on reverent feet for it was either dead or about to die, and would therefore be free of holiday makers in their yearly madness. It balanced its wooden houses and wooden shops and wooden church on grassy slopes which fell to a pearly beach, and stood its single solid brick pub on level ground above all: and here on most days in the week, for it was usually either too hot or too rough for fishing which was an exact science in Oomallunga, the men of the place could be found drinking and talking and practicing their personalities. I drew pictures of the town and of those of them who would pay for the pleasure, and spent what I earned on drink and food in that order. At night I slept beneath the crooked Tea Trees which fringed the beach and my days would have been as carefree as the bird's except that my brain was on fire with a great secret which the men of Oomallunga had told me.

They spoke of a Monster, a Sea Beast so repulsive to look upon that none who had seen it were alive to tell the tale. In their grandfather's time it would often rise out of the sea roaring with terribly fury, and send great waves at the shore which crushed their boats and broke their nets and kept them in their houses or The Pub for weeks on end. All their grandfathers were dead and only an old woman had since seen its tail above the surface and was blind and dumb from that day. So for me he was a second hand Monster and each hand coloured him with a new horror. I listened to them all and found a strange pride that this beast of our southern seas could out-monster the most monsterish beasts which ever roared in northern climes. The men of Oomallunga had missed this point, but they doubled up with laughter and agreed it was so when I brought it to their notice. They often laughed; for they were a simple folk and delighted in simple things.

But best of all, and this is what lay me on the beach dreaming when I should have been drawing for a fee, was the reason why The Beast was never seen or even heard of outside this one small Australian fishing village; and why he had sent the grandfathers to their graves and apart from the unlucky dame seemed to have lost interest in their offspring for two generations; it was treasure. When the man with sandy whiskers and clear blue eyes told me about it in The Pub all his friends nodded their heads and agreed it was treasure. Enough wealth to buy half the world, they said. The man with sandy whiskers told me exactly where it was, and they all agreed with him that word for word these were the directions their grandfathers had told them. About half a mile out in The Inlet and thirty fathoms down there was a long high rocky ridge. At a certain point along the base of this ridge was a hole which was the opening of a tunnel; and this tunnel went down another ten fathoms until it curved up under and into the ridge itself. There it opened out into a large cavern which had at its furthest end a wide ledge, and at the back of this ledge was the treasure; and around the treasure, snarling and rumbling and roaring, lay curled the terrible, unheard of, Oomallunga Monster.

Needless to say I made it appear that talk of treasure did not greatly interest me, and said that what had been too much for their grandfathers was more than enough for me. Offhandedly I pointed out the big weakness in their directions, which was how over all that water to fix the exact position of the hole. A little man with a harelip said that was easy, that on the first of January every year a Sea Hawk with one withered leg hovered over the spot until its shadow was thrown on the very place, then it flew away not to be seen again until the following year; or so his grandfather had said and he died the most painful death of all. The simple men of Oomallunga laughed themselves silly at the memory of this, and the little man ordered drinks all round, for it was the festive season with two days to go until The New Year.

So I lay on the beach and looked out over the water, and its steady swell was breathing in the deep and the glint of sun on its surface was gold and jewels at its heart. Soon I would have to act and I had very little to go on, for there are no standard works on dealing with Sea Monsters and lurid descriptions were no substitute for living habits, weaknesses, and the best means of attack. The Thing slept on a ledge coiled about the treasure, and both were contained in a large underwater cavern; that, apart from the directions, was all I could rely on, the rest I should have to reason out for myself.

I reasoned that the Monster was probably a Mammal because its task of guarding something required an elementary intelligence, in which case the cavern should be ventilated. If this were so then I could dispense with elaborate breathing gear and improvise something for a short journey. Having settled fundamental, I turned to the directions I had been given and found that I did not place too great a faith in the accuracy of their detail. Probably the thirty fathoms down to the hole was accurate for the men of Oomallunga knew their working stretch of water, but the length of the tunnel to the cavern, given as ten fathoms, was almost certainly wide of the mark. So I set myself twenty fathoms for the tunnel and hoped for less. All of this gave me a fifty fathom swim, assuming that my return journey was not made in the same operation; it was a long way, but after a little thought I devised a simple method of ensuring my safe passage to and from the cavern whether it was ventilated or not. My next and greatest problem was how to deal with the great Sea Beast when I got there. I would need a weapon of some sort and the choice was limited by the means of getting it there; also, such things as hand grenades were ruled out, for though they would finish the job quickly with little danger to myself, they would also damage what I came to get. Finally I settled for a rifle, a knife, and a home-made spear.

Having, in my dreamy optimism, arrived safely in the cavern and accounted for The Monster, I then devised the necessary tackle for hauling my prize back to the surface; and that done, I remembered how the man with sandy whiskers had a stout rowing boat for sale, then I gave up the effort of thinking and settled further into the warm soft sand.

I lay there and blessed the simple men of Oomallunga; wise men all who could hold a secret well and who knew a man of action when he came. And so I drifted into sleep for my strength's sake, under as hot sun on the last day of the year.

Part 2

On the first morning of the new year I awoke beneath my favourite tree with not a penny left to me in the world, and my heart gone wild with keenest expectation. I stood and stretched in the sharp air and a great pity came over me for all men who slept their nights in beds and dozed their days in worn familiar paths. I opened my last bottle of Burgundy and drank to the year and to all people everywhere, and especially those of Oomallunga; then, as I did every morning of the summer, I raced to the highest place on the cliffs behind me and sang and shouted at the point of dawning. I called The Sun a loafer, a lazy good-for-nothing, taunted and cajoled him, dared him to show his face above the world and account for where he'd been. Then at the first sight of his shamed and blushing cheeks, I laughed with joy at his confusion and raced him to the water's edge, plunging beneath the crisp small waves before his first red hand came grasping at the beach.

I swam and dived and rolled and splashed before walking into the quickly warming day. Then I stood beside my new things; my good boat smelling of fresh paint and salt and linseed, and inside it, neatly arranged and ready for use the following items:- One sixty yard length of rope tied at one end to a large rock: one thirty yard length attached to a heavy hook: one sixty yard length of narrow rubber tubing attached by twine to another rock and to that end of it I had fitted a rubber sucker and stopped the opening with a cork: A .303 Repeater with three spare clips wrapped in oilskin: my large hunting knife and a spear I had made from a broomstick and a carving knife: a powerful waterproofed torch which I could strap onto my head like a miner's lamp: two deflated car tyres and a hand pump: and a big canvas bag also wrapped in oilskin and containing sandwiches and a water bottle, shirt, shorts, socks, and a heavy pair of boots. These necessities had taken all my money and a bit over, yet I was immensely pleased with every one of them for I fancied that not once, by word or sign, had I given any hint to the merchants of Oomallunga of the real reason for their use.

I had been assured that The Sea Hawk never appeared before 10 am, so I had ample time to stride over once more through the streets of the village and eat a large breakfast which was owing to me at The Pub. I laughed back at the many small boys who hailed me that way from their houses, then at 9.30 am, I slipped quietly back to the beach and slid my boat into the water.

With long strong strokes I pulled her past the headland that shielded my beach from Oomallunga Jetty. I looked back and saw most of the local men gathered there for some private purpose, and they waved to me and shouted words across the water which sank before they reached me. I was not sorry to be gone alone upon my great adventure.

The water was so clear that I soon picked up the beginning of the underwater ridge, and I observed how as the depth increased its upper surface became jagged and uneven. I rowed along it until its features were obscured and it became no more than a darkening of the water, but I also kept my eye on an imaginary line I had drawn the previous day, joining two points on opposite sides of The Inlet itself, and which I calculated would cross The Ridge about half a mile from the shore. When I arrived at this point I began the difficult task of holding my boat stationary against the outgoing tide, making the final preparation of my gear, and continually scanning the sky for sight of the mysterious bird. Then it came upon me how utterly dependent I was upon this bird, and how, even though its yearly mission argued something of the supernatural, it was not impossible for natural causes to remove it from its course. As I waited and. the minutes stretched into hours and the sun climbed higher and higher in the sky, I became convinced that I was the victim of a cruel hoax. I saw providence laughing as the men or Oomallunga had laughed, not like them in simple humour, but with cruel malice at having led a fool to his undoing. I saw the search for gold as an unworthy one, and I reflected on the fate of those who had pursued it before me; but I would rather have met death in the deeps below than have come so far and returned unharmed because of an empty sky. In the waste of water I had to have a marker, and I had to have it whilst there was still light to guide me down to the ridge below. I knelt in the boat and prayed for a sign. I would give all my wealth to charity; I would live a life of sacrifice and love for all man; I would be nothing and the doing of good deeds would be all; I pleaded like the weak creature I was before The Almighty; I beat my breast at my own unworthiness and rose with tears in my eyes to observe a hovering speck in the far blue sky.

It circled round and round fixing its own positions, then it descended turning its ominous head from one side to the other. I watched it with a fever in my blood and my heart throbbing in my throat, and I shouted with joy when I saw its one red leg stretched beneath it and the other a stump hanging useless in its flight. Suddenly it dropped upon the water and when I thrust the oars in deep and leaped towards it, it rose screaming and was gone from my sight within the second; but I had marked my spot and when I was over it I threw out the heavy anchor and made ready for the great dive below.

My preparations were quickly done. First I made one end of the rubber tube fast to the boat so that its opening could not be blocked in any way, then I dropped the other with its rock overboard. I was pleased to feel it strike bottom before being fully extended. Next I fastened the long rope to the stern and dropped its rock over: I had thus ensured a means of breathing before entering the tunnel and provided a way of returning to the boat if I was heavily laden. Then I strapped the torch to my head and the rifle spear and canvas bag to my back. I fixed my knife about my waist and tied the tyres and pump to my thigh, and coiling the hooked rope about my shoulders I grasped the one at the stern, breathed deeply of the summer air, and stepped beneath the surface of the sea.

As the water closed over my head and I felt the first breathless impact of the cold, fear sprang from my soul to my body and shook me. Had I not been holding my breath I would have cried aloud and scrambled back into my boat and raced away from this awful place; but as I opened my eyes in the green glass and felt the smooth rope sliding through my hands and the thud of pressure against my ears, the discipline of a lifetime quelled the fear and down I went hand over hand, passing into a seaweed world of razor rock and waving arms. Then I saw rising before me the grey bulk of the ridge, its surface glowing with a white phosphorescence; and it grew before me until I could not see its peak and all my sight was filled with rock and water. I was so overcome by my own insignificance in face of this casual immensity, that my feet were standing on the sandy floor before I realised my desperate need of air. Carefully I expelled my breath as I stumbled and floated to my rubber tube. I pressed the sucker over my mouth, withdrew the cork with my teeth and sucked in breath after breath until the hammering stopped behind my eyes and quiet confidence returned to my mind.

The first step of my adventure had been taken and I was at the point at no return; then I saw it. There was a rock as big as an elephant which stood out from the ridge and behind it was the opening. It looked no more than a blackness against the grey, roughly triangular in shape and covered with the beckoning limbs of sea ferns, and as I surveyed it I felt coldness prickle at the back of my neck for I fancied that behind that screen, unseen eyes were watching me. I took a last deep breath, replaced the cork, unsheathed my knife, and swam towards it.

As I parted the ferns my heart stopped beating, for something enormous and moving in all its parts blocked my path, I switched on my torch and kept going, and as the light stabbed the blackness a thousand small fish, for that was all it was, rushed around me to the open water; their sharp scaly bodies beating against me and driving me against the smooth wall of the tunnel before I was alone again, and much relieved to continue my journey I had been badly scared but my own determination pleased me greatly; and I reflected that all monsters everywhere are no more frightening than the human courage with which they are attacked.

To my surprise I found that swimming through the tunnel was both easier and harder than I expected; easier in that there was a slight current running with me, and harder because as it sloped downward I kept bumping my head and scraping my back against the roof. The fact of the current lifted my spirits to a peak of optimism for it meant that the water was going somewhere, and supported my belief in an airy cavern. The force of the currant increased as the tunnel became narrower until at its smallest diameter, which was about fifteen feet, I was racing along; then suddenly, when I had been swimming for about four minutes and desperately needed air, I found my face against smooth rock and realised that the tunnel had turned upward and that I had come up into a funnel and that there was a surface of water above me. I knew that at last I had entered the ancient home of the Oomallunga Monster. I can remember to this day how frantic I was for breath; how I longed to slice up through the veil and explode my lungs in the welcome air but a warning bell was jangling in my brain. I saw myself flapping helplessly from the water on to some rocky shelf, and being incapable of any action beyond that of breathing whilst The Thing, whatever it was, finished my hopes and myself at its leisure; so I slowed my rush to the surface, and somehow managing to gain a toe-hold on the glassy wall of the funnel, I unscrewed the connection from the hand pump at my thigh. With this simple breathing tube I was soon ready to face what no living human eye had ever seen. The water about me was some degrees warmer than that in the tunnel, and, as my breathing returned to normal my whole being became more composed than at any time since I awoke that morning. I unslung the rifle in its oilskin wrapping and the spear, and I loosened my knife in its sheath; then I slowly raised my head above the surface.

I was not sorry to see what I saw, though I confess it was something of an anticlimax, for of living breathing life there was no sign at all; though in every other way the cavern was breathtaking in its proportions. Fully a hundred feet high and sixty feet across it stretched before me like some mighty temple. The back wall of the funnel rose sheer behind me to become its end, and in front the water spilled out over a rocky ledge some five yards wide before it tumbled down a drop of four feet into a stream bed that ran down and away before me. This stream gave the cavern its most memorable feature, for it did not flow smoothly but at evenly spaced intervals it dropped away again keeping level with the descending floor of the place; and at every drop it sent a cloud or steamy spray into the air so that I imagined myself in some gigantic turkish bath. The walls and roof were barely discernible in this mist, but they gave off the strange white phosphorescent light which penetrated the atmosphere and was broken up into a multitude of colours, so that I seemed to be in the heart of an all embracing rainbow.

I rose out of the water and stood enraptured on the slippery edge. Then slowly at first, then with an overpowering urgency I felt drawn to run leaping over the stepped floor down into the mouth of all the beauty. But there crashed into my head a warning: this was no place for human enjoyment, it was a hot steamy temple of evil. The way down beckoned and called and pulled at my limbs which I felt becoming sluggish in the awful humidity, and drowsiness was leaning on my eyes. After my exertions in the water I wanted to go down into that warm centre and sleep and sleep and never wake again. Then friendly fear shook me and I knew I must go up.

There was a gallery; I saw it running up the left hand wall some fifteen feet off the floor, and. I knew that somewhere up there I would find the cool source of air. I scrambled, slipped and splashed beneath it and swinging my hooked rope like a lasso I sent it upwards. I thanked God when the hook caught fast and I was able to pull myself up the sheer face of wall and clamber onto the damp surface of the gallery. It was no more than two feet wide but I went along it on my hands and knees, so relieved to be rising out of the evil fog that I had no thought at all for the perilous drop which brushed at the edge of my right hand. Higher and higher I climbed, and the air became cooler and sweeter until at last I looked down upon the great foaming bath of colour which had almost been my grave.

Then the gallery widened and I was able to walk along it comfortably, and since it was out of the mist the going was firmer and I made good speed. Before long I felt the welcome need of food and. sleep so I looked for a cavity in the wall, and to my joy I found one. It was a true find for it was in fact a small cave with a low wall at its entrance; deep enough for me to lie snugly down inside it and be out of sight from the cavern. I went in and spread my things about me. First I unwrapped the rifle and leant it against the front wall with my spear and knife beside it, then I changed into my dry clothes. I opened my sandwiches and water bottle and. feasted better than a king, and when hunger and thirst were gone I lay down warm in the dry air, and fell into a deep sleep.

Part 3

As I slept I dreamed the strangest dream. I dreamed I saw an hour and it grew into a day, and I dreamed I saw a day and it grew into a week; and at the end of the week I dreamed I saw the waters of the Oomallunga Inlet and over the waters the men of Oomallunga drew my small boat, and there were hard sad looks on their faces. And I saw myself swimming beside them and shouting at them to stop and to take my boat back, but they could not hear me; because instead of words there came from my mouth clouds of rainbow vapour. I swam and swam until my limbs ached with exhaustion and perspiration poured from every part of me but I could not keep up with them; further and further I dropped behind until I gave up the chase and from a distance watched them pull my boat up on the beach. Then I saw the women of Oomallunga file slowly down to the beach and they were wailing and moaning for one who was lost to the sea. And when the men made to touch them and comfort them they lifted their faces contorted with bitter rage and hissed at them, their fathers and husbands and sons, and closed their eyes tight so they could not see them. And I felt an awful trembling come over me for it seemed they were hissing and shutting their eyes from me as I awoke, sick with terror, in the cavern beneath the waters of The Oomallunga Inlet. My eyes were open; there was sweat in the palms of my hands; still I could not feel the fear; and still I could hear the hissing.

It came from outside my small cave. I drew the rifle down beside me and released the safety catch, then I turned on my knees and looked out over the wall.

At first the cavern looked the same as when I had gone to sleep, but as my eyes became accustomed to the light I picked out a moving object in the mist below me; a huge indistinct blue-grey thing which swayed back and forward in the swirling colour, and there rose from it the chilling hiss and moan of the women in my dream. I watched it coming towards me from the furthest end of the cavern and my imagination was appalled at its size; for this could only be the head of the thing and the rest or it moved slowly over the floor which was more than fifty feet below me. Quickly and carefully I strapped all but my rifle about me. I made some noise doing this and immediately the creature came more directly at me, then, when it was no more than twenty yards away though still below and shrouded in mist, it stopped moving and the hissing increased in volume. So we stayed for some minutes, The Oomallunga Monster and I, and I was almost believing that it was as afraid of me as I was of it, when the deafening hiss changed to an angry barking roar and it raised its head out of the steaming cloud.

Even now as I write this in my old age, I feel physically sick at the memory of that sight. The blue-grey skin so long under the phosphorescent light had become transparent, and where it was not underlaid with bone, I could see all its pulsing moving parts. Its head was shaped like that of a great bird except that it had no forehead and its boney crown continued to a point like an upper beak; its lower jawbone formed an under beak and both were lined with a continuous ridge of cruel serrated bone. From the centre of its crown to the point or its upper beak there ran a saw-toothed crest of bone, and on either side of this crest, protruding in transparent flesh, were its eyes and nostrils. The nostrils were not set close to its head but were more like long feelers, dilating and stretching and slapping against the beak, and every time they opened I heard the frightening hiss. I judged the beast to blind from the movement of its eyes. These were milky blue with the smallest grey slit in each to indicate a pupil; they were completely lidless and revolved round on their fleshy stems independently of each other, and with a desperate sightless urgency. This head was six or seven times my own size, but it seemed ridiculously small on the long transparent neck which stretched down into the coloured mist, so that I could not tell if it walked on legs or was in the shape of an enormous snake.

I knew it would be foolish to waste bullets on bone in an attempt at its brain, so I aimed at the converging bunch of nerves at the top of its neck. I was about to pull the trigger when the beast made its first lightning strike. Faster than any snake it crashed its boney crest against the gallery some twelve yards to my left, and I thanked God for the cave as my passage ahead split away into the cavern below. As it swung its head bask I fired but I knew I was wide of the mark. The Thing screamed in pain and rage and I saw one of its eyes shatter as though it was marble, and blood pumped down its beak. Again it crashed its head at the gallery, to the right of me; and this time the ledge before me as well crumbled away and thundered down into the mist. Shocked into panic I fired three times at the head as it swung back then what I hoped for happened: it paused uncertainly out there, groaning and hissing. I aimed and shot into the bunch of nerves but I was trembling so much that I hit it wide of the centre. The Monster dropped suddenly from my sight and I heard it scrambling and splashing its way back along the cavern floor. Then all was still again and I was alone in my cave, frightened and shaking with no means of escape.

As I regained control of myself I made a startling discovery; I found there was fully a week's growth of hair on my face. So my dream was at least partially true and my sleep in this eerie place had been beyond all expectation. No doubt my boat would he gone from The Inlet as the ledge was gone before me, and the people of Oomallunga would have given me up for lost; but as I still had some food and water left I reflected ruefully that things may well have been worse. Then I experienced one of those strange moods of confidence which any man who has stood at the end of adversity will recognise, that anything that could possibly happen was bound to be an improvement. I counted my blessings. Firstly I was still unharmed and I had wounded my adversary, and secondly I knew something of the nature of the Monster; and fear which is rooted in knowledge is never half so bad as that which rides wild on the back of ignorance. So I comforted myself with these thoughts then I considered my next move.

A search of my cave produced nothing but bare unbroken rock so my first move was obvious; I would have to descend, if I could, to the cavern floor. Supposing I got there at my own pace, then there would be two courses open to me; either to meet and battle with The Monster on its own ground or try and make my escape back through than tunnel to the sea, against the current all the way. In this case escape was just as dangerous as combat for there would be no boat waiting for me if I did get to the surface, only a half mile swim in whatever weather prevailed before I reached the shore. On the other hand if I killed The Monster I could then search for another exit at my leisure; the source of the air for example. I knew if I remained inactive too long that fear would return and I would never go down at all, so I quickly tightened my gear about me and finished my food and drink; then I fixed the hook of my rope so that I could shake it down to me if I reached the floor and still in that strange method of confidence I began the descent.

It was easier than I expected. At thirty feet I found another gallery so I made a fresh pitch with my rope and this time I felt it reach the floor. Also I found that my long rest had given me extra resistance to the steamy fog, so that I reached the cavern floor still fresh, and very satisfied with the progress I had made. I decided the best route to follow would be along the wall to the far end of the cavern rather than the more direct path of the stream, for down there the heat and humidity were at their worst: so I set out and soon discovered that thoughts of The Monster were put right out of my head by the dangers of the path I had taken to its lair.

The fall of rook caused by the destruction of the upper gallery had only added to a breaking up which had gone on for years, so I had to test every step I took, and several times an apparently solid surface crumbled to white dust under my weight and I had to struggle hard to avoid being smothered. At other times I had to traverse smooth wide shelves which were as slippery as ice; but I advanced at the cost of broken nails and many cuts and bruises, and though I made much more noise than I intended, at the end of two hours I judged I was half a mile nearer my quarry.

The rainbow mist was my greatest problem it made all obstacles seem much closer than they were; and it blurred outlines so that I frequently thought The Monster was upon me and recoiled from nothing but oddly shaped boulders. Then suddenly the mist ceased, as though it had been sliced through with a knife, and I saw I was at the end of my journey.

Before me there was a lake of jet blank water which stretched for about three hundred yards to the end wall of the cavern. It was in the shape of a half circle with the wall as its diameter and in the centre of this wall was the ledge I sought. Raised like a huge smooth stage its edges dropped a sheer fifteen feet into the water, and there as I had been told I would find it, was the whole awful moving mass of The Oomallunga Monster.

Part 4

For a time I stood on the bare rock between mist and water, so overcome by the terrible task before me that I was incapable of constructive thought or action. Then I became aware that my shirt was flapping against me and I realised why the fog was rolled back off the lake: somewhere ahead was the source of air and from it a breeze blew. It not only gave me sight again, but best of all it kept my scent from going out across the water. My luck was surely in, for even at that distance I could see the nostrils of the beast straining and slapping against its beak in a vain effort to detect me. Also I could see that its lower body was like that of an enormous seal, except that its two flippers were more like webbed claws and its tail went on forever, and that it seemed to be trembling all over as its head swayed from side to sides on the end of that hosepipe neck.

To shoot at it from where I stood was out of the question, for a shot that was not instantly fatal would give my position away; so my last move in this deadly game would have to be more perilous than any yet; I would have to swim the lake and take what chances came my way on the other side. In complete silence I blew up both the tyres and rested upon the water, then I strapped my gear to them and holding my rifle above my head I slid into the lake.

The water was warm about me as the minutes past and I came closer and closer to the ledge. It was a long tiring business, but gradually the ancient beast above me grew to fantastic proportions and I saw that it was desperately aware of approaching danger. Not for a single instant did I take my eyes from that moving head, for I knew that if its wounds permitted and if it caught either sound or smell of me, it would be off the ledge and on me in the water before I could raise a finger to save myself. So my progress was slow, only a deep movement of my feet propelled me, and breathlessly silent; but inch by inch I advanced, and still the great head swayed and the one eye rolled, and the searching nostrils slapped against the beak.

In a corner of my eye I saw that the ledge did not rise sheer, but along its length it overhung the water by about four yards; and that ahead of me at water level was a small rocky outcrop, which if I could reach it, would give me firm ground to stand on. It meant that The Monster would be cut off from my view, but it is the way with all of us to lose sight of a great danger in the pursuit of some immediate goal; and so it was with me. Soon I was stepping up my speed, eager to be out of the water: and maybe it was providence which led me to commit this folly, I do not know, but finally I made it, and hardly daring to breath I rolled onto dry rock and gave fervent thanks for being once more on my own element.

The next part of my adventure moved with incredible swiftness from the instant I stood upright on the rock with my rifle and spear in my hands, to the proud moment when I was alone on the upper ledge.

I remember I had a plan of somehow climbing on to the ledge and shooting up into the beast's brain from underneath, and I was about to act on this when I saw the terrible mistake that I had made: for as I stood there in the dry air the stream rose from my wet body and it was too late to halt the message that it carried. Then I heard the hissing increase in volume and felt the rock around me tremble as the thing moved its great bulk towards the edge. About fifty yards to my left I saw its head swing down until the tip of its beak brushed against the water, and its nostrils were slapping and its breath blew furrows in the inky surface. Then the sickening sight swung in, like a huge pendulum, until the underside of its lower jaw touched the rising wall. In this manner it came towards me swinging and slapping and hissing, and all my confidence in being on my feet again and my pride at having come so far left me, and I gazed in the paralysis of terror at the approaching end of everything.

I tried to raise my rifle and my arms would not answer; instead I felt it slip from my fingers and afar off I heard it clatter on the rock beneath me and splash into the water. My eyes were held staring by its one sightless eye which revolved above me and around me and did not see me and still the thing came on. Then it was upon me; swinging out in an agony of hours and I knew that this time there was no hope, that I would first be crushed against the wall and beyond that I dared not think. I saw it start towards me and suddenly my limbs were freed and I moved. For an instant I felt blank surprise that my rough-made spear was still in my hands, then I stood straight up with my back pressed against the wall, and I closed my eyes and held this knife bound to a broomstick out before me.

We touched, The Oomallunga Monster and I, and for an eternal second I felt the cold rough softness of the skin flap under its lower jaw before the whole cavern pealed to its agonised scream and my spear was torn out of my hands. The Beast rose slowly writhing and turning in the air in a great leap from the ledge, and I had one sight of my broom-handle quivering from its neck and the knife set firm in the bleeding nerve centre before its whole bulk plunged deep down into the lake. I saw a huge wave rolling at me then I was lifted from my rock with all the breath knocked out of me; I remember striking my head on the overhanging ledge, then burning blackness filled me.

I must have been unconscious for some hours for when I awoke my clothes were bone dry. I looked about hardly believing my luck for I was on the ledge itself and around me, as though they were the remains of a wreck washed on the shore, were my two tyres and all my gear. My head ached and there was a roaring in my ears which I thought at first came from within me, then I looked out over the jet blank water and saw a sight which I shall never forget; for the water began to foam and bubble, then it heaved and its surface split open and the great beast was drawn up out at it, still writhing and turning and vainly trying to shake from its neck the dart that was its death. Again it plunged into the depths and the water rose over the ledge but it did not reach me.

So for hour after hour I crouched there unmoving, and watched it fight its lonely battle out over the inky water. Each successive leap was lower than the last and each time the dive was deeper and the wait longer; and in my heart I was sorry for what I had done and yearned to bring the poor thing back to the ledge and take my unworthy weapon from its neck; but I could no nothing. I exulted in every leap and tensed through the time of every dive; until I knew the end was near. Then, after the longest dive or all, I saw the black lake move again and I knew I would soon be alone.

The water surged and foamed aside and saw such a sight, that the dragging weight of sorrow lifted from me and I stood on the ledge and cheered; for the creature came with mighty power and its last leap was higher and straighter than before. Nor did it twist in the air but turned slowly over at the peak of its climb and seemed to hang suspended near the very roof of the cavern, as it would look for the last time at its ancient home; then with noble ease it curved its swan-like neck and dived straight and true into the bottomless lake. And as I watched it spear down through inky water, so clean that it left scarcely a ripple on the surface, I knew in some unfathomable way that The Oomallunga Monster had won its fight with death.

I found the treasure where the grandfathers of Oomallunga had said it would be; a great quantity of jewels and precious metals beyond counting and beyond price, and I did not question then as I do not question now, either how or why it came to be there. That it was there for the taking was sufficient and I had no doubts but that I deserved it, so I packed the cream of all I found into my large canvas bag and strapped this with my other things to the two tyres. Then I made a brief exploration of the ledge.

Two things I found there are worthy of mention but one of them, because I delight in a mystery, I shall forget to tell you until the end of my story. The other was a pitiful collection of human bones which I judged to be the remains of three men, and over them I spent some time in sorrow and prayer before giving thanks that I had not added to their number. Then I gave them Christian burial, and with a last look at my most exciting find and the great pile of treasure still renaming, I entered the water and began the journey back.

My return to the point where I could climb again to the lower gallery was difficult but uneventful, and with the need for caution gone I made excellent speed. I hauled myself up to it then set out hoping to prove a theory I had regarding the ventilation of the cavern; for I reasoned that both upper and lower galleries had been formed over the years by the passage of air over the rocky walls. This meant that they should converge at the source of the air, and it was there I hoped to find a way back to the sun.

And so it proved to be; but for my purpose here I prefer to gloss over the awful perils I encountered after I found it. How I climbed for endless hours in a treacherous damp dark shaft; scaling impossible heights and bridging depths where echoed the murmur of the world, before I saw a light in the distance and knew that rest was near. And how exhaustion claimed me with the end in sight and I slept bound to an outcrop of rock with the whole shaft beneath me; only to be awakened by huge rats which had almost gnawed through the rope: these things are a story in themselves. I need only say that eventually I stood on dry ground under a burning blue sky; then I left a hole inside a hill so cunningly concealed by nature that I doubt if even I could find it again, and took: my bearings for the my back to Oomallunga.

Part 5

I did not return immediately to The Inlet but first spent some weeks in another town where I was not known, and where no questions were asked about my scarcely human appearance. There I exchanged some of my small gold pieces and bought new clothes and much good food and drink, which set me up as a man again. I rested and regained my strength, and finally with my heart filled with gratitude for the good men of Oomallunga who had generously given me their secret, I set out to repay them for their kindness.

I arrived in their town on a Saturday afternoon when I knew that all the men of the place would be drinking in the pub and hanging on the phone for the race results. In the old days I had been one of them, drinking and laughing and sketching and betting and solving all the world's problems in the diplomacy of beer, but this time it was different. I stood outside the bar and could not enter for a great fear had come upon me; a fear of the fact that these were proud independent men who would spurn the gifts I brought them; a fear of the change in me. No longer was I one for them to laugh at and pat on the back and repay a drawing with a pint of bitter; for now I was rich beyond all their dreams and my gratitude would be condescension and my gifts an insult to their pride. So I stood there trembling;

listening to their noisy laughter and their harsh voices and the clink of glasses, and I smelt the hot sweaty smell of their dinking before I steadied my courage and pushed through the door.

Slowly everything stopped. Silence. Heads turned towards me. Eyes, frightened eyes stared at me. I shook off the silence and laughed for them. I walked towards them and they backed away. I banged money on the bar and shouted that the drinks were on me, and some of them blinked and shuffled and they looked at each other and I felt the tension move. "Drinks on me." I shouted again "As much as you want and more for I've killed your Oomallunga Monster."

Over and over I repeated it, and as the dinks lined up along the bar I saw fear give way to disbelief and that to uncertainty, and finally someone began to laugh and it grew into a flood which roared at me from every side. I could not be heard above the din, though I shouted and stamped my feet and banged on the bar for silence; still they laughed. They pointed at me and slapped their thighs and held each other for support and only paused to drink the beer I bought; then suddenly my ears were opened and I heard their laughter for what it was, and always been. I looked deep into their red faces and saw something more terrible that any beast which lives beneath the sea, for on the lips of these men there was mockery and in their eyes contempt. Something precious died within me and the world fell from under my feet.

The man with sandy whiskers wiped tears from his eyes and asked me what I took him for; and were they all fools like me to let me turn the joke back on themselves. I heard his words as though they were another dream and I was back in the eerie cavern; how there never was an Oomallunga Monster, and never would be; how it was all a huge joke of their grandfathers to send the unwanted stranger on his way to look for treasure and a one-legged bird, and bets were laid as to whether he would take the bait or not; and how they had done the same and rid themselves of many a one who had overstayed his welcome, though none had ever staged a more dramatic exit than mine. To swim out of The Inlet and leave the boat with its rope and rubber tube was a great touch, he said, but to come back dressed like a millionaire and try to play the game out was the best of all. Then the man with the harelip pointed at me and said I looked so sick and silly it made him cry, they all roared again; beside themselves with laughter.

I shrank away from them, within myself, and turned from them and buried my head in my arms, and rode out my private storm of sorrow. As though visible emotion was a great marvel they stilled their jeers before it and I heard them move uneasily behind me.

I could not believe my ears. These "benefactors'" of mine were wrong about something bigger than a mountain and I had the proof in my pocket. Somewhere along the line a cynic had lived amongst them dry enough to shrink a wonder to a jest and they had believed him. Wild thoughts these and others spun in my brain then slowly stilled before a vision of human bones on a ledge in a cavern, far beneath the sea. And I felt my sorrow melt in burning anger which turned me around again and pressed against my eyes and shook my voice with feeling.

"Murderers!" I screamed "You killed three men. Three strangers the same as me you sent beneath the water, and when they left your evil disbelief they found that what was false was true."

The men of Oomallunga fell back before me. I continued in a whisper and none of them dared disturb me. "There was a cavern and I reached it; a noble monster and I killed it; treasure and I found it; and I returned to find friends but I have not found them; only liars in a house of lies."

They watched me scarcely daring to breathe as I brought from my pocket a leather bag and tipped its gleaming contents into my left hand. I selected the smallest gold piece that was there and held it up in the sunlight so that it smiled foolishly at them. I saw their eyes possess it and felt their gaze, soaked with greed, tighten at my finger-tips; and again I spoke softly.

"I came back to you bearing a rich reward but now you shall not have it; except this one piece, the least valuable of all, to prove to you I have not lied." I dropped it in the slops and dirt on the floor and they made to move then stopped. Slowly I poured the sparkling stones and other precious things back into the leather bag and drew the string tight about its neck; then I walked to the door and paused inside it. "With what is here," I said, "I will raise a. monument to this town; a caution to every stranger who comes along the road to Oomallunga. The price of your disbelief." And as the door closed behind me and I hurried away from that place I heard them falling like hungry dogs upon the gold and fighting for its possession.

I bought land beside the road at the head of the cliffs and on it I erected a statue of a man draped in sea ferns and standing over the dead body of a strange sea beast. And his outstretched arm pointing back down the road and away from the town; and I inscribed it "To The Memory Of There Strangers." Then, after this was done, I went forever from the men and the town and the waters of The Oomallunga Inlet.

Part 6

One thing remains to tell before I end the story, for I saw many wondrous sights in my great adventure and the passing years have hung them in my memory like pictures sleeping, except this one; which breathes and moves and challenges me still. Alone I fought an ancient monster and won a mighty prize; but it is not that. And still I see its awful head rising from the rainbow mist; and the steamy glowing cavern and the terraced river and the jet-black lake, and the ledge and the human bones, and the huge beast in its last sad dive; but it is none of these things It is that other discovery I made when I explored the ledge; for in a deep hole scraped out of the rock and lined with warm seaweed and sand, and three times as big as myself, I found an egg.

Let those who are brave for fortune find it as they may; bur if there be any who would tread the path I trod, I caution them to remember one thing; that it is fifty years ago today since all this happened.

THE END

TRAP STREET

Trap Street is a FREE Australian *Doctor Who* e-zine, co-edited by Dallas Jones and Roger Reynolds. It is planned to come out regularly, approximately every 4 months.

So far issue 1 and a special Series 10 Survey issue have been released. Issue 2 will be available very shortly.

All you have to do to get each issue of **Trap Street** is to be put on our mailing list so that you can be advised when each issue comes out and how to obtain it. To do this send an email to: editors@drproductionsaus.org

Please include in your email your name, your email address and, if you are from Australia, your state, or if from another country, then your country.

DOCTOR WHO CLUB OF AUSTRALIA

As a DWCA member you get access to

4 issues of the club's print magazine Data Extract
Exclusive digital publications such as Zerinza and comics
Merchandise pre-ordering through the DWCA Shop
Discounts at select retail outlets
Discounted entry to select third-party events
Advance notice of DWCA events
Access to exclusive competitions

There is also the chance to meet Doctor Who celebrities, with the **DWCA** having hosted events with many of the programme's stars over the years. These have included Peter Davison, Colin Baker, Sylvester McCoy, Louise Jameson, Camille Coduri, Frazer Hines, Elisabeth Sladen, Nicholas Courtney, and our club patron, Katy Manning.

But the soul of the **DWCA** are our members and we want to hear from you - we hold day events across the nation every month, have an active Facebook page, fantastic book club, trivia nights with amazing prizes and if you have a talent or a passion - we're eager to showcase it in publications like these!

We're 40 years young and we've only got there through regeneration. Every single person who contributes to the **DWCA** is a fan, so no matter where you live, young or old, the **DWCA** is here for you.

Members pour their hearts and countless hours of free time into the **DWCA** in recognition of the hard work and effort of every member that came before us. Members that made sure that when we became fans we felt welcome.

So if you've never attended a **DWCA** event or know a fan who isn't a member - just remember it's easy to make friends here as each and every one of us have something in common.

WE LOVE DOCTOR WHO
www.drwhoaustralia.org

Printed in Great Britain
by Amazon